STILLNESS

DAILY GIFTS OF SOLITUDE

RICHARD MAHLER

Red Wheel

Boston, MA / York Beach, ME

First published in 2003 by Red Wheel/Weiser, LLC
York Beach, ME
With offices at:
368 Congress Street, Boston, MA 02210
www.redwheelweiser.com

Library of Congress Cataloging-in-Publication Data
Mahler, Richard.
    Stillness : daily gifts of solitude / Richard Mahler.
       p. cm.
    Includes bibliographical references.
    ISBN 1-59003-042-7 (alk. paper)
    1. Spiritual life. 2. Silence—Religious aspects. 3.
Solitude—Religious aspects. 4. Conduct of life. 5. Silence.
6. Solitude. I. Title.
    BL628.2 .M34 2003
    291.4'3—dc21

                                    2002152831

Typeset in Bembo
Design by Joyce C. Weston
Printed in the United States of America
RRD

10 09 08 07 06 05 04 03
 8 7 6 5 4 3 2 1

CONTENTS

ACKNOWLEDGMENTS

My deepest appreciation goes to Grove Burnett and Linda Velarde who, with the assistance of their children, Cisco and Maya, enabled me to spend three months in silence and solitude amid the magnificent landscape of northern New Mexico. I could not have had this experience without the wide-ranging support of Kate Droney, who read early versions of this manuscript and gave me valuable feedback. Others who offered their suggestions and insights after reading parts of the manuscript include Jan Johnson (my editor at Red Wheel/ Weiser), Jill Rogers, Nicky Leach, Mollie Seymour, Suzanne Kryder, Paul Ingles, Richard Sherwood, Nancy Avedisian, Dan Shemp, Niki FitzCallaghan, Connie Goldman, and Charlie Luthin. Literary agents Gareth Esersky and Joanna Hurley also provided helpful guidance and advice.

For providing time and space to write, I am indebted to Ann Muriel, Paul Zalis, Barbara Lemmick, Mark Setterland, and both the Tim Chappell and Mike O'Connor families.

My heartfelt appreciation is also extended to Saki Santorelli, whose strong words of encouragement kept this project going; to Sue Dirksen, who introduced me to the rewards of meditation; and to Niki FitzCallaghan, who extended greatly needed support at a critical juncture. Above all, I extend deep and profound thanks to Nicky Leach, who understood the importance of this book and believed in it as passionately as I did, generously providing priceless emotional and wise editorial support during the work's challenging gestation. Others who were particularly helpful in times of need were Courtney Best Trujillo, Daniel Bruce, Gail Ackerman, and Jon Kabat-Zinn. Thanks also to the participants in my mindfulness-based stress reduction courses, who certainly taught me as much as I taught them. Finally, I wish to thank my parents, Don Mahler and the late Mary Mahler, who instilled in me a deep love for silence and solitude.

STILLNESS

CHAPTER ONE

INTO THE QUIET

Silence is golden.
— Traditional saying

I magine the epitome of "peace and quiet." Maybe it is somewhere you have been before: a palm-shaded beach or a mountain lake encircled by pine trees. Perhaps it is a cozy room in your home where you can stretch out on a comfortable couch to read a good book or take a nap. It could be a trail where you walk your dog, a secluded meadow that's perfect for a picnic, or a spa that offers hot tubs and mineral wraps. Maybe your ideal destination for the embrace of silence and solitude is a place you have not yet visited, except in your imagination.

I began writing this book one year after I disappeared into the snow-covered Tusas Mountains of northern New Mexico. My solitary confinement was voluntary, and I entered this chilly exile after weeks of careful deliberation and planning. Like naturalist writer Henry David Thoreau at Walden Pond in the 1840s, I went to the woods to live "deliberately." Echoing Thoreau, I wanted "to front only the essential facts of life, and to see if I could learn what [silence and solitude] had to teach, and not, when I came to die, discover that I had not lived."

FEBRUARY 12—DAY 25

My heart aches with the magnificent beauty of this stunning wilderness. Today is my forty-seventh birthday and I feel like I am eighteen, facing a life overflowing with possibilities, each more exciting than the next. In this still, calm, silent place, I have found my center and my balance. My life has never felt better.

I began this diary, as a way to understand my isolation, seven weeks before my seclusion began and continued making entries for a full year following my return. These readings represent the raw material of my experience. Their shifts in tone and focus reflect the internal changes I underwent.

DEC. 1—48 DAYS BEFORE DEPARTURE

I have decided to embark on a personal odyssey of discovery. For at least ninety days I will be living alone at a ranch tucked in a high mountain valley of northern New Mexico. The ranch is in the Tusas range, an extension of the San Juan Mountains of the Southern Rockies, about thirty miles south of Colorado and fifty miles west of Taos. I will be roughly eight miles—as the raven flies—from the nearest paved road and about five miles from the closest neighbor. My home will be a snug, pitched-roof, three-bedroom house that lacks the usual amenities of modern civilization. My only connection to the "outside" world will be via a radio-linked telephone (for once-a-week calls to verify my well-being) and the occasional visits of my employers. Am I ready for this? Absolutely! I can hardly wait for the adventure to begin.

My job as winter caretaker was to prevent vandalism or unauthorized entry to the ranch, which was otherwise only occupied during warm months. My presence was a precaution in the unlikely event that someone would find their way to the end of the gated, unmarked dirt road leading to this hidden location. Nestled in a narrow valley at nearly nine thousand feet above sea level, the fenced property was generally left alone during winter, when snowdrifts blocked all incoming roads and even the nearest highway was often closed by inclement weather. During the fourteen weeks of my residence, I had plenty of time to ski, snowshoe, read, write, and consider the age-old question, "Who am I?"

I learned, among other things, that a time of quiet reflection and contemplation can be a great teacher. My life was altered by the interior transformation that took place during my isolation. It took a year for me to realize the true depth and scope of these internal changes, and to be able to describe them in words. I have felt a strong desire to share some of what I observed and learned. My experience of silence and solitude suggests others can benefit from their transformative powers.

I approached my extended time of silence and solitude with an open mind, a porous heart, and a spirit of excited optimism. Any wisdom I accrued during the course of my wilderness sojourn was experiential. Although my rational mind shaped this extended retreat, what I learned came through doing it. And, to an even greater degree, I was affected by the "nondoing" of a great many activities I would otherwise have engaged in. The paradox of simultaneously doing and nondoing, striving to learn and letting learning simply happen, is a source of the potency that resides within silence and solitude.

I hope to help readers explore what psychoanalyst Ester Schaler Bucholz in *The Call of Solitude* calls "quiet alone-time." A wider appreciation of quietude may embolden and enrich your life in unimaginable ways. You may not have a realistic chance of experiencing in the extreme sort of dropping out that I indulged in. Few among us are able (or willing) to rearrange our lives to disappear from sight for ninety-seven days. Yet each of us *does* have the power to embrace a focused and purposeful silence in our own daily lives, if only for a few minutes at a time.

Terry Tempest Williams, who writes with fluency and passion about nature, love, and culture, captures the healing essence of quiet alone-time in her book, *Desert Quartet: An Erotic Landscape:* "To find a place of rest and safety, no matter how fleeting it may be, no matter how illusory, is to regain composure and locate bearings." Williams, who lives in a sparsely populated corner of Utah, finds refuge not only in the silent desert landscapes near her home, but in the art museums and galleries of large cities, where she may be surrounded by scores of people at a time. She embodies my conviction that we can access the transformative qualities of silence and stillness even amid noise and movement. Like me, Terry Tempest Williams has learned that one also may be unconventional in pursuit of solitude, finding the essence of aloneness within rather than through physical estrangement from others.

Each of your idiosyncratic paths is sure to be different. I hope to inspire you to move outside a habituated daily routine that may have "disconnected" you from yourself to one that better reflects your innermost needs and desires. I will prompt you to be more creative and thoughtful in how you realign (or even reinvent) your life.

Since my extended foray into the mountains, I have made quiet alone-time a small but deliberate part of my day. The consequences of this decision have astonished me. I reflected on some of these discoveries in my journal, a year after coming back to the city from my time in the woods:

APRIL 21—365 DAYS AFTER MY RETURN

They are little things, but they add up: keeping the radio off in the car when I am driving by myself, or going outside for a few moments on a nice afternoon to sit still in the sun, where I listen to the melody of a bird and the whisper of a breeze. When it is cold or I have had an

exasperating day, I may take a hot bath, with bath salts and a candle
glowing nearby. During warm weather, I arise before dawn, watching
the slow bloom of colors in the east and feeling the fresh, bracing
coolness of the morning air.

Most of the time, after taking such breaks, I am calm and
revitalized. My concentration is more focused and the demands of
my life feel less overwhelming. Bringing myself back into balance, I
am in less danger of toppling over. My jaw relaxes and my chest
softens. The simple act of closing my eyes and breathing deeply for
a few minutes, even in front of my humming and hungry computer,
reduces my stress level and makes my schedule more manageable.
I've gotten so used to making these kinds of "mid-course
corrections" during my day that I cannot imagine life without them—
and wouldn't want to.

My withdrawal into wilderness came at a time of great personal turmoil. My five-year relationship with a woman I loved was disintegrating.
We had known this truth for months, but were reluctant to face it. The
situation was confusing, since we were still good friends and shared my
house. We wanted to move forward emotionally, but didn't know how.
The inner conflict was paralyzing and demoralizing.

The emotions felt familiar. About nine years earlier, I had reached a
similar crossroads in my professional life. For ten years I had been a self-
employed journalist and teacher, based in Los Angeles. I was weary of the
financial uncertainties of freelancing and I was dissatisfied with what I
was doing. Much of my work involved reporting on the mass media and
show business celebrities, subjects that no longer engaged me. I was ready
for a major shift, but unclear what path to follow. I did feel, however, a
strong and focused desire for more downtime and privacy. Stuck each day
in a brain-numbing commute on the Santa Monica Freeway, I yearned
for long, unstructured days to reflect on my life and the changes I might
make as I moved forward. At the time, such feelings were more intuitive
than conscious. Unmarried, healthy, and childless, I had enough money
in the bank to meet my needs for a while. I was in a good position to take
time off. With my life in low-level turmoil, I needed to do so or run the
risk of becoming more dissatisfied and of developing stress-related health
problems.

In 1988, I drove away from my fast-lane life and relocated to northern New Mexico, where the lanes are not only slower, they are often

unpaved. I had family and friends in the area and had spent time there over the years. I had bought a house in anticipation of my move, which would shift me into a new life as a full-time independent writer, teacher, and radio producer.

Despite the intrinsic uncertainty of my new career, I noticed a host of positive results that I attributed to my relocation: lower blood pressure, happier disposition, renewed interest in work, more rewarding relations with family members, the stimulation of new friendships, and a greater enjoyment of life and its simple pleasures. Nine years later I was ready for another change, albeit less dramatic. This is what led me to be alone for so long in an alpine cabin.

DECEMBER 15—34 DAYS BEFORE DEPARTURE

I'm a little scared about doing this, mostly because of what's unknown to me. I have never been alone for three weeks, let alone three months. My most relevant experiences have involved extended travel (where I've been "psychologically" alone for a month or more at a time) and Buddhist meditation retreats (where I've twice been in silence for a week at a time, and three times lived briefly as a solitary hermit).

I feel no fear about the actual aloneness of this experience. Indeed, I'm hopeful and intrigued. More than anything, I feel ripe. I anticipate feeling much more "unstuck"—more finely tuned and tightly focused—when this experience is through. Beyond that, I don't want to make predictions or try to "frame" what is to come, lest the experience be skewed by my attachment to a particular outcome. This is harder to do than I first thought, however. I keep feeling myself leaning into the future, making elaborate plans in my head about what I expect to do and how I anticipate this retreat will affect me. It seems ironic that even when I yearn to do "nothing," I feel compelled to "do" something with that nothingness. This is the way humans drive themselves crazy.

The embrace of silence and solitude cannot begin to address all the conflicts and problems spawned by our noisy, hectic lifestyles. Nonetheless, we can enlist them as creative allies in a personal campaign to create simpler, more balanced, less frenetic lives. When used effectively, even a little silence and solitude can go a long way toward restoring vibrant health and a strong sense of well-being. New England writer May Sarton, who lived alone much of her life, once observed to Connie

Goldman on her 1989 radio show, *Too Busy to Talk Now*, that "everything that slows us down and forces patience, everything that sets us back into the slow cycles of nature, is a help."

I reflect on Sarton's words as I gaze out my studio window. The converted garage has large windows on two walls and a door that opens onto the courtyard garden that surrounds my home. During the course of a year, I observe the cycles of nature as they unfold. As I write this, the snows of winter have melted, revealing the first pale green leaves of spring. The shoots of buried bulbs are popping up, and a few of these plants are already blooming.

The return of flowering bulbs always seems like a miracle to me. In the depths of a snowy January, it seems impossible that they will survive. Yet only eight weeks later, they are radiant with resurrected life. This restoration emerges in its own time. The bulbs know nothing of deadlines and urgency; they simply follow the dictates of nature and the vagaries of weather. They conserve and store their energy until conditions are exactly suited for them to bloom. If the plants rush themselves, perhaps taking advantage of an unseasonable winter thaw, they may be injured fatally. In a similar fashion, our human hurrying and anxiety does not get us where we want to go any faster. In fact, the opposite may be true. When I take a few quiet moments to look out my window, seeing the simple truths that plants "know" naturally, the urge to cram too much into a single day often evaporates.

If you are like me, your urge to "be productive" is difficult to resist, particularly when thousands of clever gadgets and customized services seduce us into "doing" ever more. It's ironic that much of the technology we have developed to make our lives easier has the opposite effect. Even with the "help" of microwave ovens, overnight delivery, cellular telephones, hand-held computers, fast-food restaurants, automatic teller machines, and e-mail, many of us complain that our lives are still too rushed and too full.

Are you ready to join me in a softer, less frantic way of life, an existence that's simpler, yet offers more? Each of us can achieve this. It starts by slowing down and paying attention to the world around us, as well as listening to our innermost voices. When we really see, feel, and hear what is going on inside us—within our hearts—the necessary changes can begin. But first we do well to help the distracting exterior clamor to subside.

JOURNAL ENTRIES, FIRST THROUGH EIGHTH DAYS OF MY RETREAT

JANUARY 18

I notice the sky and the light much more here than in the city. And always the silence. It is big and tangible, like an ocean that holds my small voice in its immensity, a tiny boat unseen beyond the endless horizon or beneath the slow swells.

JANUARY 19

The silence is deafening, even ominous at times. When I step outside, it hits me like a hammer, refusing to be ignored. The only signs of life are Steller's jays in the aspen trees and flies buzzing along the windowsills. The unstructured day takes getting used to; I sometimes stop completely and ask myself, "What happens next?" But no one is here to answer me, and my own reply feels feeble and inadequate.

JANUARY 26

I'm getting used to the isolation but find myself having conversations in my head. It would be nice to have someone to talk to once in a while. The nights are the worst. But in the silence I also notice the infrequent sounds of wildlife. Yesterday and today I heard the drumming of a hidden grouse. A splendid owl hooted yesterday at sunset. A coyote barked—exactly like a dog—at the woodpile a few days ago.

To gauge the full measure of silence and solitude, it is useful to know how uncommon these states of being really are—and how this scarcity affects us. With more than seven billion humans on our finite planet, noise and congestion are nearly inescapable. Without our realizing it, crowdedness and unwanted sound distance us from the precious domains that lie within our bodies and souls. Part of the challenge of being fully human today is learning to accommodate, manage, and respond to this turbulent sea of sound. We dismiss or ignore it at our peril.

STOP TO LISTEN

Whenever I take time to close my eyes and listen—really listen—to the immediate environment around me, I am surprised by what I hear. Although I live in a small, nonindustrial city, my neighborhood is awash in sounds I neither make nor desire: wailing sirens, buzzing saws, clattering garbage trucks, thumping boom boxes, and ringing school bells. The backdrop, at least on weekdays, is the low hum of the city itself: the undistinguished and submerged sounds of its traffic, commerce, and distant voices. I am used to this clatter and do not think about it much, unless a noise becomes unusually loud and aggravating. Some sounds, like bird songs and the laughter of children, are even comforting. Mostly, however, the noises I live with are simply the aural equivalent of wallpaper, to be accepted as unchangeable, for better or worse.

When you close your eyes and really tune into where you are, what do you hear? And how does it affect you? Take a moment now to close your eyes and listen—really listen—to the sounds around you.

Sounds shape more than our moods and feelings; they contribute to the many ways we think about and react to our surroundings. We all have been annoyed by the sound of a loud motorcycle, shrieking car alarm, or whining toddler. Yet these distractions are only a small part of the ever-growing and uncontrolled loudness of the world as a whole—from which there often appears to be no relief. With our Earth adding thousands of new people each day, it is no surprise that opportunities to enjoy solitude (and escape noise) have almost vanished altogether.

I did not realize how rare it is to be *completely* quiet and alone until my tenure as caretaker of the New Mexico ranch. There I found silence of the blood-pounding-in-your-ears variety. After a few weeks, the human voice became a vague memory. Absent the din and distraction of urban life, I found a calmness and serenity that, paradoxically, was also invigorating and uplifting. I felt focused and healthy, happier than I could remember feeling in years.

JANUARY 27—DAY 9

My days are satisfying and full, even without the many urban distractions—from mail to movies—that I still sometimes miss. At night, when the winds are calm, the silence is complete and enveloping. The land feels asleep and at rest. Those creatures that stir during the day—including me—are curled up in their warm burrows or hiding places. And the starry sky is stunning. I have discovered the small but intense pleasures of this simple life. Despite my privations, I feel remarkably content.

SOUND HEALTH

Clinical studies confirm a host of measurable benefits that can result from spending even a small amount of time abiding quietly in our own company. They include a sharper memory, less irritability, quicker reaction time, improved concentration, more efficient breathing, deeper relaxation, an easing of depression, and better sleep.

Besides preserving our hearing, an embrace of silence and solitude also may reduce anger, tension, and stress. It is the last of these that may have the greatest potential impact on our physical health. High stress levels are commonplace in modern society and contribute to the current epidemic of "lifestyle diseases" that kill millions each year. Chronic stress compromises the proper functioning of our immune systems and increases our susceptibility to a broad range of debilitating illnesses and conditions, including heart disease, hypertension, arrhythmia, cancer, headache, back pain, chronic anxiety, insomnia, depression, chronic fatigue, irritability, and eating or digestive disorders.

Unfortunately, din and distraction exact their toll without our awareness of the damage. Studies confirm that stress hormones, pulse rates, and blood pressure rise in response to certain kinds of noise, even when we are asleep. Think you've gotten used to the background hubbub? Clinical research suggests otherwise.

According to the League for the Hard of Hearing, continued exposure to loud noise has a negative impact on cognitive development, social behavior, and learning. Between 1982 and 2000, the League screened 64,000 Americans and found that hearing loss had increased from 15 percent to 60 percent in all age categories. A separate League survey identified vehicles, motorcycles, airplanes, and helicopters as the most common sources of disturbing noise.

When I returned to the "outside," the first thing I noticed was how much agitated activity and seductive distraction we encounter in the course of a typical day. On the way back to town, my employer stopped at a gas station minimarket shortly after leaving the ranch, and I felt over-whelmed to the point of paralysis by the products on display, the blaring radio, the exhaust fumes, and the ill-humored purposefulness of the constant stream of customers.

What I was reacting to was the simple reality of modern life. Everywhere we go, "loud and busy" confronts us, constantly attempting to undermine any impulse toward "quiet and slow." Public places, in particular, have become the bought-and-sold terrain of advertisers and marketers, who huckster us without mercy. No wonder Americans are the most anxious people on Earth, spending billions of dollars annually on prescription drugs and medical care aimed at alleviating stress-related disorders. It comes as no surprise that we are forced to tune the world out, both literally and figuratively.

Writer and hospice counselor Stephen Levine describes in *Planet Steward* the anxious energy of urban life as a force conspiring to keep us out of tune with other more healthful resonances, to our detriment. "Large cities produce an unnatural modulation inharmonic with the human body, tuned through evolution to the planet, which makes it difficult to stay centered," Levine writes. "If the rhythm of the individual becomes that of the dynamo of the city, he will literally go out of his mind. . . . So it becomes necessary to rebalance."

A respite from the hurly-burly not only feels soothing, it is good for us: psychologically, physically, intellectually, emotionally, and spiritually. We know that an overly pressurized and scheduled life is not healthy. The physiological consequences of living this way are probably more far-reaching than we imagine. Yet each of us can make significant lifestyle changes—like finding ways to enjoy silence and solitude with regularity—that make it easier to cope with debilitating aspects of the rat race that are tough to avoid. A yearning for occasional quiet alone-time may be instinctive.

"Man cannot long survive without air, water, and sleep," notes anthropologist Thomas Szasz, in his book, *The Second Sin.* "Next in importance comes food. And close on its heels, solitude."

This hunger for personal silence comes as no surprise to social scientists. They know that throughout most of human history, a serene life was the norm. Some of the loudest noises our ancestors heard were a clap of thunder, the whistle of a bamboo flute, or the honk of a goose. At night, people were lulled to sleep by a serenade of crickets or the sigh of rustling leaves. Over thousands of years, humans developed a communication pattern and a speaking volume rendered obsolete by urbanization and technology. In remote parts of the American Southwest, where I live, one still encounters the old way of soft speech among members of the Navajo and other indigenous tribes, who sometimes talk so quietly that outsiders have difficulty understanding them.

"Our ears are not made for a noisy world—they're made for spoken communication, which occurs at a level far below what we experience in the streets or at the airport," Jochen Schacht, a professor of biological chemistry at the University of Michigan's Kresge Hearing Research Institute confirmed in a 1999 interview with *Cooking Light* magazine. "The fact that we are losing our hearing is no more surprising than if we were losing our sight by looking at the sun."

Even when we recognize the negative impact of excessive movement and clamor, their effects are insidious. Have you ever felt so overtired from stimulation and activity that you were unaware of your own exhaustion? I feel this way during the crunch of work deadlines or the hectic pace of holidays. I remember also, first as a teenager and later as a college student, stepping into the cool night air after attending an ear-splitting rock concert and not until that precise moment realizing what a terrible headache and psychic pounding I was enduring. I still feel the same numb, mind-clenched sensation after a long flight on an airplane, where the sound of jet engines is inescapable.

But seeking refuge in silence is not simply the body's healing response to physical noise. As humans, we also need a break from the psychological demands of interaction and reactive activity, which create a different kind of noise within our heads and hearts.

Psychiatrist Anthony Storr, in his groundbreaking study, *Solitude: A Return to the Self,* concludes that "some development of the capacity to be alone is necessary if the brain is to function at its best and if the individual is to fulfill his [or her] highest potential. Human beings easily become alienated from their own deepest needs and feelings. Learning, thinking, innovation, and maintaining contact with one's own inner world are all facilitated by solitude." In other words, getting *away* from it all helps us get *close* to it all. If we are constantly subjected to *outside* stimulation, we cannot respond to stimuli *inside*.

The seventeenth-century French scientist and philosopher Blaise Pascal took this idea a step further when he concluded that "all the evil in the world" stemmed from the inability of the average man or woman to abide silently in his or her own company. Pascal's view was extreme, but it underscores the valid view that we are likely to be more at peace with ourselves when we occasionally stop to sit quietly and attentively. Within this undefined interior space we can make appropriate decisions about how best to spend, in the words of Mary Oliver's poem, "The Summer Day," our "one wild and precious life."

THE BODY'S HEALTH-AFFIRMING RESPONSE
TO QUIET ALONE-TIME

Silence and solitude practices—meditation and yoga, for example—have positive effects on the body and mind. For instance, a study cited in a 2000 issue of the American Heart Association's journal, *Stroke,* noted that a reduction in stress—even without changes in diet and exercise—can reduce the risk of heart attack and stroke. Relaxation through meditation can reduce symptoms of atherosclerosis, a common cause of strokes. Similar studies support other conclusions based on a regular embrace of quiet alone-time (see Recommended Sources).

- More and better sleep, less incidence of insomnia and other sleep-related disorders.
- Improved general health and slowing of some aging processes.
- Sense of well-being and contentment.
- Lower incidence of hypertension, mental problems, and heart disease.
- Easing of headaches, depression, anxiety, panic attacks, muscle tension, and back pain.
- Greater self-control and less inclination toward anger.
- Increased productivity, better memory, and improved ability to concentrate.
- Less absenteeism from work and school.
- Stronger immune system and more available energy.
- Lower heart rate and greater blood flow.
- Reduced risk of heart attack and stroke and possibly a reduced incidence of certain cancers.
- Some evidence of reduction in addictive or obsessive behaviors.
- Aid in treatment of psoriasis, sleep disorders, and a variety of other health-related problems.

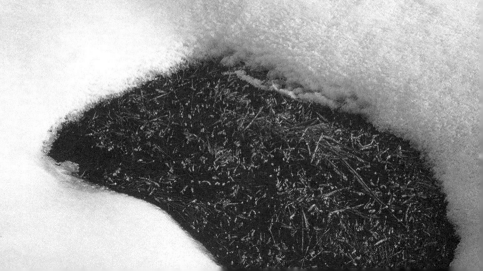

CHAPTER TWO

RETREAT, REEXAMINE, AND RECONNECT

It is a great relief when, for a few moments in the day, we can retire to our chamber and be completely true to ourselves. It leavens the rest of our hours.

—Henry David Thoreau, *Walden*

When my cat Chumley feels threatened by overeager dogs and hyperactive children, she heads for the farthest closet and hides until the coast is clear. Not a bad idea under such circumstances. All animals, including Homo sapiens, act on a natural impulse—a survival response developed over millennia—when they withdraw during times of severe stress and rapid change.

Like kitties, when humans face difficult or overwhelming situations, our inclination is to hide in a safe place to gather strength, process information, or problem-solve. A quiet refuge is where we lick our wounds, gain perspective, and establish priorities. In safety and stillness our intuition comes to the fore, allowing us to follow a gut feeling or reasoned strategy about what choice is best. One distinct value of withdrawing to a calm, undisturbed place is the development of inner strengths that can be directed toward whatever crisis is at hand. In this way, we acquire some imagination, skill, and elasticity for handling life's inevitable tensions and losses, traumas and challenges.

In the same spirit people have often used quiet alone-time to reconnect with themselves, to discover a special kind of knowledge and high quality of insight that is difficult to acquire amid the cacophony and clutter of the average person's daily life. This was true centuries ago, though we tend to regard the past as a simpler and easier time. Peter France, in his retrospective book *Hermits: The Insights of Solitude,* notes that the devout early Christians known as Desert Fathers (or Anchorites) found their self-imposed exile in isolated Egyptian monasteries brought them "not merely an escape from distraction . . . [but] a teaching presence. To remain silent and alone is to be open to influences that are crowded out of an occupied life." In France's view, "self-knowledge can only come through solitude." While this may be an overstatement for some, history suggests it is resoundingly true for many.

In contrast to the slow, serene world of full-time spiritual seekers, the Information Age has forced many to conform to the lightning-speed processing of the computer, which is now integral to almost every device or service we use. We unwittingly believe humans should perform like microchips: fast, efficient, consistent, multitalented, and available twenty-four hours a day, seven days a week. Computers—along with cell phones, cheap airfare, powerful cars, instant messaging, and other pre-sumed amenities—have infected us with a sense of unbridled urgency. Many of us have internalized "computer time" to the point where we become irritated and impatient if a person does not respond right away to our phone message, fax, page, or e-mail. The chronic nagging is trans-ferred to everyone within striking distance, frazzling nerves throughout our breathless society.

But a machine-based timetable is hardly a natural pace for people—or other living things. We may have forgotten that the five-day workweek to which most of us adhere evolved during the Industrial Revolution as a way of meeting the demands of mechanization. The nine-to-five sched-ule is unknown in tribal societies. Anthropological studies suggest that most hunter-gatherers who preceded us only needed to spend three to five hours each day satisfying their essential needs, using the rest of their time for leisure, contemplation, making art, or group-involved cultural activities and spiritual rituals.

Many of our more immediate ancestors were, a century ago, follow-ing the cycles of the seasons and watching the weather as they tilled their fields, fed their livestock, and tended their orchards. Even in those days, people tried to do too much. An important difference, according to scholars, is that their "doing" was more often counterbalanced by calm moments of introspection and deliberate "nondoing." By nondoing, I suggest taking time to let your body and mind feel at ease. This means coming to complete rest: not knitting, not watching TV, not talking on the phone, not reading, not taking a walk—not engaging any other pur-poseful activity.

This is not a new idea. For thousands of years, the spiritual leaders of all great religious traditions have advocated regular intervals of slowing down or stopping. Christian and Jewish traditions ask the faithful to cease work and recharge for one day each week. Through ritual, prayer, chant, dance, music, reading scripture, and other contemplative activities, renewal of the human spirit remains a priority within most spiritual practices, even for adherents whose lives are filled with other activities.

Senator Joseph Lieberman, for example, takes a deliberate inward journey one full day each week. According to syndicated columnist Betsy Taylor in the September 2000 edition of the New York *Daily News,* Lieberman does not drive a car, turn on the TV, or go shopping. While

Lieberman does this for religious reasons—as an Orthodox Jew—he might agree that striking a balance between one's professional obligations and personal needs is important. For most of us, it is hard to imagine what our lives would be like if we deviated from our routines the way Lieberman and thousands of his faith do on each Jewish Sabbath.

Although I follow no particular religion, my intention to keep personal alone-time in my daily life has been made stronger and more viable by studying the role of silence and solitude in various faiths. In Christianity, for example, Jesus set an example by retreating to wilderness areas to pray and reflect. "Solitude transforms," wrote pyschotherapist and former Catholic priest David Kundtz, in *Stopping: How to Be Still When You Have to Keep Going.* "When you come from a time of aloneness, you are a different you." Buddhists have placed meditation, generally in silence, at the heart of their spiritual practice and see its rewards as transformative. Kundtz quotes Insight Meditation Society director Edwin Kelley: "Silence is one of the simplest, most valuable relaxation tools we have." Similar observations have been made repeatedly by adherents of the Islamic, Jewish, Hindu, Confucian, and Taoist faiths, among others.

Why then, despite such unequivocal support among our spiritual leaders and practitioners, are silence and solitude so hard to find? How could qualities that once were so much a part of daily human life become so rare?

My own response is twofold. First, I see silence and solitude crowded out by our consumption-oriented society, driven by a fast-paced economy that demands much of our attention—and more with each passing day. Second, we simply do not value silence and solitude enough.

We love our state-of-the-art amusements and conveniences. Thanks to sophisticated technology, there is no limit to the ways we can now entertain ourselves: from personal communication devices to fancy cars, from digital movies to Internet websites, from gourmet restaurants to high-tech fitness centers, from overseas vacations to mind-altering drugs. Of course, we (or those we love) labor long hours to pay for all this—and strive to find a little leftover time and energy for spouse and children, relatives and friends, church and neighborhood. While we earn the money to support our active lifestyles, our big houses and spacious apartments sit empty much of the time, and our expensive cars rest in parking lots where we work.

FINDING TIME AND SPACE BETWEEN TASKS

Given the pace of our lives, it's amazing we are as healthy and happy as we are. Somehow, we manage to find time for what we find most important: organizing a successful birthday party for a son or daughter, treating a loved one to a special meal and intimate conversation, taking care of an elderly parent, and meeting critical deadlines at work. Yet many of us would also like more of these precious events in our busy lives.

In the course of juggling our calendars, we can find brief intervals where quiet alone-time thrives. Here are a few examples, but feel free to add your own:

- *Turn off the telephone and hang up a "Do Not Disturb" sign for a while, using your office, yard, balcony, or bedroom as a refuge.*

- *Go to work early—or stay late—so you can center yourself before—or after—the details of your day predominate. With more "big tasks" under control, you can focus more on smaller demands like finishing a phone call before doing something else or dealing with a coworker's question directly.*

- *Leave a few minutes early for your next appointment; use the extra time to find a little stillness within yourself.*

- *Close your eyes and take deep breaths when you move from one task to another. This restores your balance and helps you let go of any tension associated with the task you're disconnecting from.*

- *If you use a computer, turn it off—all the way off—so you can experience life without the insistent hum of this electronic taskmaster.*

- *Get up and take a walk—even for five minutes—as a way to rejuvenate your mind and body. Find a pleasant place to stop—such as a park—during your walk.*

We trade silence and solitude away for other activities that involve making noise, being busy, or experiencing the company of others. Many of us have spent so little time being quiet and alone that we do not know what silence and solitude are really like, so we never consider them important.

Other observers have drawn their own conclusions to explain the absence of quiet alone-time. "Most of us find it easier to read about solitude than to practice it," notes David Douglas in his memoir, *Wilderness*

Sojourn: Notes in the Desert Silence. "There is a stigma attached to being alone. Solitude, often seen as a twilight province of eccentrics and misanthropes, is suspect. This social taint, as much as the specter of danger, works to discourage solitary excursions. . . . We hear of acquaintances who have gone alone for a few days to the desert or mountain, and our first response is likely to be a solicitous query: 'What's wrong with them?'"

The prevailing assumption is that a life of constant social interaction is not only normal, but essential. Our cities and suburbs are set up to accommodate this common view, and the rise of instant-access communications has made constant connectedness a reality. Yet it wasn't that long ago that even long-distance telephone calls were an expensive luxury, and "snail mail" the norm. As a society, we are struggling to catch up with an ever-faster pace of life.

Indeed, today's lifestyles and attitudes are an enormous contrast to those encountered in earlier eras. I recall the story of Ishi, a Native American who walked out of his homeland forest in Northern California in 1911 and was discovered to be the very last member of his tribe (see Recommended Sources). The fortyish man had lived the previous five years completely alone in the wild before a shortage of game had spurred him to join "modern civilization." Ishi became an object of anthropological study and public curiosity, living the rest of his days at a museum in San Francisco's Golden Gate Park.

One aspect of Ishi's reaction to this odd existence was that he remained fascinated by crowds and fearful of loud noises, neither of which he had previously experienced. Taken to an opera house for the first time, Ishi ignored the talented and elaborately-costumed singers on stage and spent much of the evening staring at his fellow patrons. He explained later that he had never imagined so many people could fit into such a small space. Today, few of us can conceive of the kind of life Ishi enjoyed in the wilderness, immersed in silence and solitude. Yet there may be a part of ourselves, operating below our conscious mind, that yearns to experience fundamental aspects of such a life, just as Ishi continued to miss his nature-oriented existence for the five years he felt "captive" by an urban society. (He died, lonely and inconsolably sad, of tuberculosis in 1916.) Although Ishi was an extreme—and poignant—example of someone who could not integrate disparate cultural elements, his unsuccessful attempt to adapt to "modern life" may serve as a warning about our relentless move toward more—not less—human artifice.

THE BUSINESS OF AMERICA IS BEING BUSY

- During the late 1990s, University of Maryland researchers found that 48 percent of low to middle-income Americans surveyed said they would give up a day's pay each week if they could receive a day of free time in return. Seventy percent of those who earned more said they would make the same trade-off.

- In 1998, a Yankelovich Partners study found that one in three adults questioned said they would exchange a smaller paycheck for a simpler lifestyle. The largest group in favor of this trade (41 percent) was comprised of those aged thirty-five to forty-nine, those in the middle of their prime working and parenting years.

- In 2002, an Associated Press article reported that between 1969 and 1989 Americans added 163 hours (four extra weeks) per year to their workloads. U.S. employees now work about ten more days per year than their counterparts in Japan, who worked more than Americans until the mid-1980s. The average American now works two months longer each year than the average German.

- The same Associated Press article also stated that after the first year on the job, the average U.S. worker enjoys nine days of paid vacation (although the law does not require employers to provide any paid vacation whatsoever). Workers in Spain and France get thirty paid days off, in Ireland twenty-eight days, and in Japan twenty-five days, in all cases backed up by law.

- A 1999 Gallup poll showed that many Americans on vacation don't leave work behind. More than one-third of those surveyed made calls to their offices while on holiday, 19 percent checked their e-mail, 17 percent worked instead of played, and 11 percent cut their vacations short because of work-related demands.

For years, I was one of those workaholics that the above statistics describe. I spent a decade advancing my career as a big-city journalist, spending countless nights and weekends doing freelance work in addition to my demanding full-time job as the bureau chief for a national magazine. My life was a classic example of what stress experts call "multitasking behavior," typified by doing several activities at once without giving full attention to any—sometimes referred to in the business world as "being efficient." I experienced how easy it is to get sucked into a vicious cycle from which it feels impossible to escape. Like many of my peers, I figured the money, prestige, and professional accomplishments were worth it.

Then one day, after struggling to meet a series of intense deadlines for my work-obsessed editor, I realized that I did not know how I felt about my life. Was I happy? The easy, automatic response would have been, "Of course I am!" But the evidence was meager. My work absorbed me from 7:30 A.M. to 6:30 P.M. At night I often attended job-related functions. Many weekends were also devoted to work. One or more times each month I flew to a distant city to gather and report the news about an industry I no longer cared about. I felt I had little choice but to continue, even though I had long since forgotten exactly why a reporter's peripatetic life was so important to me. My excuse was that such an extraordinary commitment was "expected" by my employer and "necessary" if I was to remain competitive with equally compulsive journalists at other publications.

As a result of similar compulsions, millions cope with the unsettling sensation that their lives are speeding ahead too fast, careening out of their control. Days, weeks, even years fly by too quickly. Spirits sag and healthy constitutions break. In my case, growing dissatisfaction with a high-stress job and hard-charging lifestyle prompted me to walk away from it all and drastically downsize, becoming a self-employed journalist specializing in travel, the arts, and the environment. My income soon dropped by two-thirds, although I felt at least twice as happy for having left urban tensions behind.

If I were to make my break again, knowing what I know now, I would do a lot of things differently. For example, one need not forsake the benefits and pleasures of a busy life—including a good income, interesting work, a loving partner, an engaged family life, and satisfying leisure activities—to make room for equally enriching interludes of silence and solitude. The latter elements, which theologian Henri Nouwen once called "the furnace of transformation," not only can coexist, they may greatly enhance one another.

SEEING THROUGH A CHILD'S EYES

As we engage in the process of self-discovery, it is helpful to take a closer look not only at where we are but who we've been.

When you were a child, you knew what it was like to be silent and alone. We all did. In our innocence, we made up games and stories, played with dolls, became lost in books and daydreams, listened to music or made some of our own, talked to ourselves or invented imaginary companions. We stretched out on the lawn and watched bugs or spun daydreams. Summer days lasted forever and we felt immortal. Death, despair, and injury were alien, abstract concepts. The world was full to overflowing with possibilities.

Being still and fully open, in silence and solitude, helps us return to the sense of childlike oneness and wonder we once knew. We encounter ourselves again. In silence and solitude we begin to recapture our sense of being most fully alive. Being alone allows us to listen to our hearts, feel our spirits, and observe our minds. Aloneness encourages us to notice the smallest details of our behavior. By taking the time to watch ourselves with deliberateness, as an uninvolved bystander might, we may learn what we really love and what we dislike, what's truly important to us and what is trivial, what contributes to our pleasure and what drives us nuts, which people we want to be with and those whom we are ready to let go from our lives. In short, we come face to face with who we really are, as adults—possibly for the very first time.

Give yourself the gift of a child's delight in the marvels of our everyday world. For at least ten minutes, sit on the floor of a space you use often, such as a living room or bedroom. Look around with the eyes of a three-year-old, the eyes of wonder. Pretend you really are three. Then notice what's different about what is most real, most joyous, and most loved by you. Maybe you'll make up a story, have a chat with an imaginary friend, or invent a new game. Maybe you'll find yourself mesmerized by something you've never noticed before.

At this point you may be muttering to yourself, "Get real! It's *impossible* for me to find a time or place to be quiet and alone, except when I'm using the bathroom—*maybe!* My life is too full to add even *one* more thing, particularly sitting around gazing at my navel or pretending I'm a toddler." From such a perspective, silence and solitude are luxuries that offer such negligible benefits that it feels unrealistic to make room for them. The idea of standing still, when so much inevitably remains undone, seems not only ludicrous, but impractical or even sinful.

Some may have a self-effacing response to the suggestion that they embrace silence and solitude. "I don't have a moment to myself and I would feel guilty even asking for one," such a person might say. "I need to get permission for time alone because I don't want my spouse, family members, or employer to suffer on account of my indulgence. It would hurt their feelings if I went off by myself." From this point of view, quiet alone-time demands that we ignore others, perhaps even pushing loved ones away when they seem to need us.

Life is complicated, isn't it? Even when our goal is to simplify. I agree that if you are like me—and most people I know—your life already is filled to overflowing. It's as if there were no time to do the things we *have* to do or feel *obliged* to do, let alone *want* to do. In this too-common scenario, it is hard to know where our own desires and needs fit in, or how much of a priority they should be.

But a shift in perspective can change things. Passive navel-gazing—in the conventional, disparaging sense of that term—is not what an embrace of silence and solitude is about. Look beyond the cultural stereotype of a far-out mystic contorted into the lotus position. If you regard personal time-outs as episodes of torture or oppressive obligations, you will shun rather than embrace them. An equally plausible reality is that moments spent quietly alone may be among the most pleasurable and rewarding—and sometimes the most challenging and growth-inducing—of our entire lives. Cultivating a positive, accepting, flexible attitude toward the potential gifts of such moments will increase the likelihood that they will yield benefits.

As we discovered earlier, one does not have to be completely quiet or absolutely alone to experience the rewards of silence and solitude. We carry these qualities with us internally wherever we go. They are at the core of our being. While we may be social creatures, in the final analysis we are independent of one another, with our minds and hearts operating from an interior space that is inaccessible to others: quiet and alone.

We can learn to access our underlying silence and solitude—a birthright that comes with our humanness—whenever the need arises, even when there are people and distractions around. Embracing quiet alone-time does not have to mean leaving a job, a city, and a lifestyle, as it did for me initially. Nor does it demand the kind of extended time away that I experienced at the wilderness ranch in New Mexico. All that is required is simply disappearing "into the quiet" for a few minutes each day.

Once we make an effort to notice them, invitations to enter silence and solitude present themselves again and again, every day of our lives. Taking advantage of these moments affords us a chance to change our lives gradually, dipping into stillness a toe at a time. Notice your quiet alone-time, and pay attention.

My personal "alone-times" include the spaces between finishing one task and starting another. In a typical day, there are usually several points where I am clearly making a transition between specific obligations. Examples include a shift from paying my bills to returning phone calls, from completing a work assignment to examining the day's mail, from finishing lunch to picking up in my office again. At each of these junctures, I take a few minutes to be quiet and still. I close my eyes and take a few deep breaths, mentally releasing myself from one task or experience to be present for the next. This process can be as simple as taking a moment or two in the car after I have arrived at my destination, instead of getting out of my vehicle immediately.

I also have discovered there are many more points when I am suddenly on my own, confronted with unscheduled time. Often this is only a few minutes—as in a slow-moving line—but occasionally these unexpected breaks amount to hours or more: when an appointment is canceled, an anticipated visitor has to reschedule, or a trip demands time alone in the car, on a plane, or in a hotel room. I now take full advantage of this unexpected bonus of free time, using it to balance myself and do some inward exploration. How I go about this will depend on many things, including my mood and inclination.

There are many proven techniques for cultivating still, quiet space in even the busiest, noisiest life as a route to acquiring the kind of undisturbed personal reflection that helps us solve problems, become more creative, and gain an insightful perspective on ourselves. One of the most effective is keeping a journal of your thoughts, feelings, and observations, even if you do not consider yourself "a writer" or have never written much about (or for) yourself.

KEEPING A JOURNAL IN SILENCE AND SOLITUDE

Writing in a personal journal complements the embrace of solitude as a kind of "letter to one's self." It is a way of letting your most authentic voice be heard regularly, undiminished by the judgments of others. For some, this may be the first experience of hearing such a voice.

Because important and unexpected insights often arise when we are quiet and alone, keeping a record is a useful way of preserving our self-discoveries. This, in turn, can lead to further investigation into who we really are—emotionally, psychologically, spiritually, and intellectually. As millions of journal writers will attest, writing things down gives them a power, validity, and importance that is both liberating and provocative. In a journal, we confirm and explore aspects of our lives that we might otherwise ignore, or never even see. For some of us, this may be the only place where we are this open and honest with ourselves. As a therapeutic tool, a journal can help us chart our voyage of self-discovery over time and may itself become a valued resource for contemplation and reflection.

Keeping a journal requires nothing more than a spiral-bound notebook (like the ones you used in school), a pen, and a block of time in which to reflect and write. You can get fancy if you like, since there are all sorts of handsomely bound blank books on the market. The most important thing is to write with some regularity, preferably daily, so that you develop ready access to what you are thinking and feeling over the arc of time. This kind of listening to yourself is most effective when you make it an enjoyable habit. Even jotting impressions down—they can be fragments, quotations, or single words rather than grammatically correct sentences—will eventually result in an intriguing panorama of your interior landscape.

Many people make journal keeping an integral part of their usual quiet alone-time, when they might also meditate, do yoga, or take a walk around the block. As with these other activities, early morning is often when we are freshest and least likely to be interrupted. Still, if you find other times are better—or prefer to make journal entries on the fly—feel free to follow your own instincts.

Besides writing in your journal, remember to read it once in a while. You may make connections and gain perspectives that only come when you see your own patterns and processes over a period of weeks or months. This, in turn, may inspire you to consider new approaches to your life, or to place more emphasis on what is already serving you. The simple act of writing also may make you feel better. Research indicates that, for some people, journal keeping elevates levels of the "positive" mood chemical seratonin in the bloodstream, while simultaneously reducing feelings of depression. This finding has contributed to the growing application of "journaling" as therapy.

"Journals are an attempt to discover who you are," writer and dedicated journal keeper Jessamyn West told the *Los Angeles Times* in a 1983 interview, likening a journal to psychiatrist's couch. This is "where, without charge, one can make known by listening to oneself what the trouble is."

Personal reflective writing has proven to be an enormously helpful way of "checking in" with where I am now in my life, while providing a uniquely subjective record of where I've been already. During periods of extended personal retreat, I have noted—and expanded upon—the insights, conundrums, paradoxes, and confusions that emerge from my time alone. The process of reflection fueled by this journal writing helps me focus my thoughts and distill my emotions in a way that, in turn, allows me to see patterns, blockages, blind spots, and the sort of "Ah!" links between seemingly disparate bits of knowledge that otherwise might never reveal themselves.

My journal keeping evokes important yet submerged or forgotten memories. The writing process pulls fragments of thoughts together into recognizable forms. It brings clarity to vagueness, disposes of mental clutter, and provides a sense of resolution to loose ends. My self-reflective writing does not always lead me to definitive answers, but the very act of articulating what is going on internally makes the underlying key issues and questions of my life—and my possible responses—more friendly and accessible. Combined with the awareness wrought by my experience of silence and solitude, keeping a journal has helped me take stock of my life in a refreshing and nonthreatening way. Often the biggest surprise of my journal keeping is learning how happy I am with so many things in my life and how much of what no longer serves me I am ready to release.

MARCH 15—DAY 46

I listen to classical music and jazz all morning on the radio. These gifts of celebratory art forms are always a joy. I read, do some writing, make a few drawings. This feels like more than enough to bring a sense of gratification and delight to my day. The small, self-absorbed part of me that wants not to be here any longer is still cranky. The part that has let go of external attachments is content and serene.

Something liberating happens when certain feelings and perceptions come to the fore, when our authentic self is unmasked for us to see clearly. I call these "connect-the-dots moments." Many times there is a sense of relief, even excitement, when we become more aware of what makes us tick, even if the insights are disturbing. In the time and space we devote to this process, we are rewarded with a range of options that lead to more inquiries, conflicts, and unexplored territory. Confronting the core questions and central issues in our lives can also lead to break-throughs and revelations that are potentially life changing. We may soon discover that habits are broken, points of view shift, commitments are made, or dead weight is thrown overboard. We may stretch ourselves in ways we never imagined possible. We may reinvent ourselves like a snake shedding its skin. Who knows—we may even become more of the person we have always wanted to be.

CHAPTER THREE

LETTING GO, MAKING SPACE

A quiet hour is worth more to you than anything you can do in it.

—Sarah Orne Jewett, letter to her mentor Willa Cather

I t takes nothing to appreciate peace and quiet. But for most of us, it's been a long time since we really *did* nothing. When I was a child, I loved Saturdays. Possibilities always seemed endless, stretching from early morning cartoons on to late night rock'n'roll on the AM radio. Weekdays were dominated by school. Sundays meant church, family gatherings, and homework. But, other than the obligation to do a few chores, Saturdays belonged to me.

I grew up during the 1950s in a small town in northern California, about thirty miles east of San Francisco. Our community was tight-knit, and the worst crime was teenage drag racing on Main Street during the wee hours. When Saturday rolled around, I spent leisurely hours hanging out with neighborhood boys about my age. We played games on front lawns, built elaborate treehouses, and used scrap wood to construct "coasters" to ride down Castle Hill Road. If the weather was lousy, we might go to the matinee or play Monopoly on a living room carpet.

Looking back on those years, I realize that on most Saturdays I also found time to explore silence and solitude. I was not conscious of this choice, but it must have been deliberate. Sometimes I would find a quiet place to read a book or draw pictures. I took hikes with my dog, Wibbles, through the nearby hills that were studded with California live oaks and carpeted with wildflowers. Other times I would explore the creek that flowed near our home, its banks a jungle of overhanging trees, sinuous vines, and thick brush. I discovered early on that if my dog and I kept still and silent, we could observe wild animals—deer, raccoons, skunks, squirrels, turtles, frogs, and snakes. The rewards of quiet alone-time were self-evident.

As I grew, my Saturday pockets of silence and solitude gradually disappeared. In college, I spent weekends visiting friends, studying, reading assigned texts, or writing papers, not to mention the much-disliked task of laundry. After graduation, when I began working full-time, Saturdays and Sundays filled with the necessary errands, socializing, and unfulfilled obligations held over from weekdays. The carefree hours of youth faded to distant memory.

In recalling that era now, the spaciousness of my days seems an inconceivable luxury, given my conviction as an adult that there is always more to do than there is time. Yet in the recent past I have accepted that it will never be possible to do everything I want, and that sometimes exploring unscheduled time is the best thing for me, as it was during childhood.

"It is not merely the trivial which clutters our lives but the important as well," concluded Anne Morrow Lindbergh in her memoir, *Gift from the Sea*. Even with clutter pruned away, a full and active life offers "too many worthy activities, valuable things, and interesting people."

A critical step in the embrace of silence and solitude is setting aside the notion that we have to be "doing something" throughout our waking hours. For most of us, this goes against what we have been taught since childhood: that being active and productive is the best way to proceed. Many factors feed into this, including the strong work ethic that has shaped American culture. Everywhere we turn, there is ample praise and support for the individual who strives to "get ahead." When we are idle, by definition, we are not striving and therefore going against the grain of social imperatives.

From the outset, we must give ourselves permission to set an appointment to experience silence and solitude, setting aside the baggage of negative connotations that may be associated with "nondoing." Some may regard carving quiet alone-time out of a full agenda as a kind of cop-out. From this mindset, we are escaping reality, feeling sorry for ourselves, shirking responsibility, or, at best, wasting time. In our culture, taking time for ourselves is "not being productive." Productivity is widely praised, with little regard to its human costs.

Many of us live on tight budgets, working overtime or a taking a second job to make ends meet. With so much demanded of us for mere economic survival, stopping to experience silence and solitude may seem irresponsible at best. Living within strict financial limits, there seems no real need for introspection, thinking we know what is going on: "I'm simply trying to get by as best as I can!"

The irony is that an ongoing adoption of quiet alone-time potentially heightens awareness of what's *really* going on in our lives, which in turn may contribute directly to a balanced, healthy lifestyle and rewarding personal growth. From a purely practical standpoint, such ostensible nonactivity may "pay for itself" by helping us become more efficient, perceptive, and focused in how we spend all other waking hours. We may even become more "productive."

Looking inward does not necessarily lead to noble insight or poetic inspiration—though these may present themselves—but it usually coaxes out the significant truths of everyday existence:

"My daughter was trying to tell me something last Thursday and I didn't really hear her."

"I am happiest at work when someone comments favorably on the good job I've done."

"My stomach hurts and I get irritable when I drink too much coffee."

"I have let an important friendship wither because of laziness and neglect."

Feeling that there is some kind of payoff to exploring quiet alone-time is essential for most of us, since we tend not to go beyond the ruts of our conditioned behaviors unless we anticipate a likely benefit. This can get tricky, since the transformations we notice within the context of silence and solitude derive from the experience itself. If we get too attached to the expectation and desire for a specific outcome—"good" or "bad"—we may either ignore *other* equally informative results or influence the experience *while* it is happening to us. We need to trust that something worthy will happen, based on the reports of others and our own intuition, and plunge ahead on faith.

Despite my conviction that quiet alone-time is good for me, I still find it challenging to find time each day for a little silence and solitude. Sometimes my entire day is planned in minute-by-minute increments, with scarcely time to use the bathroom or grab a sandwich. At such times my body feels rigid with tension, even after eight hours of sleep. The last thing I want is to sit calmly with my eyes closed, performing a ritual that nonetheless has been part of my routine for many years.

I have learned that these jammed-to-overflowing days are precisely the ones during which I feel the most tangible and far-reaching effects of my quiet alone-time. Instead of turning away from this nourishing ritual, I must turn *toward* it. This effort can be very challenging when I am feeling overloaded and stressed out.

I realize I am not *taking* time to inhabit silence and solitude each day; I am *making* time for it. The distinction is important because it reflects my trust in the worthiness of what quiet alone-time provides me. If I did not truly believe that my life would be different for having made this effort, I would have abandoned it long ago. This self-assurance depends on the kind of steadfast "knowing" that one must also come to if the embrace of silence and solitude is to realize its full potential.

Breaking our cycles of rote behavior can be exhausting and frustrating. The power of long-held habits seems inexorable, as anyone knows who has tried to do something as "simple" as modifying unhealthy eating habits. Knowing this fact of human nature, it helps to embrace solitude and silence with a nonjudging mind, a light heart, and an optimistic attitude. A new ritual is unlikely to take hold the first time we try it; we may need to repeat the effort a hundred times or more before it becomes part of our daily routine.

Give yourself room to fail, recommitting again and again to your embrace of quiet alone-time—as often as necessary. Praise yourself every time you find a space that allows you to be quiet and alone—even for ten minutes—within the fullness of your busy life. Don't try to do too much, since bigger failures tend to discourage us more than small ones. Even making a tiny attempt to embrace silence and solitude is in itself a generous, healthy, and hopeful act. It is a self-loving gift that carries many ramifications. Be gentle and kind to yourself as you try to make room for contemplative stillness in your life.

"In the attitude of silence," India's pacifist reformer Mahatma Gandhi once observed, "the soul finds the path in a clearer light, and what is elusive and deceptive resolves itself into crystal clearness. Our life is a long and arduous quest after truth, and the soul requires inward restfulness to attain its true height."

We may never reach Gandhi's level of enlightenment, but each of us certainly can move a bit in his direction, even if our newfound "crystal clearness" simply involves living more attentively and with greater awareness. We can all benefit from increased self-awareness and compassion, primary gifts of quiet alone-time. When we see who we really are, through an introspective process aided by silence and solitude, we can take appropriate action.

MARCH 3—DAY 45

I'm approaching the halfway point of this adventure. My emotions are mixed. There is a big part of me that would be happy to go home right now. I miss my girlfriend, Kate, my family, my work, my house, my friends, my life. This is the part of me that dreads thinking about being here for another six and one-half weeks and that feels stir crazy. Another part of me relishes the idea of doing more of the same: bathing in silence and solitude, exploring my own psyche, going into nature every day, reading and writing by the hour, deepening my meditation practice, reflecting and contemplating. I am learning a great deal about myself in isolation, and know there is much more of great value I may soon know if I keep inhabiting this stillness.

The two impulses are not battling; they are coexisting. It is our nature as humans to have more than one motivation or desire simultaneously, along with competing attachments to past and future. These are lessons I have learned here at the ranch: that one needs to focus on what "is"—not what might be (or used to be)—and that it is possible for two or more seemingly opposed or competing feelings to occupy the same space. I can accommodate such a paradox without going nuts. This is a generous gift from this experience. Meanwhile, my feelings are raw at this point, exposed. Looking at an exquisite sunset is enough to make me cry with sad pleasure.

The embrace of silence and solitude is not without risk. We open ourselves to the unknown, which can be daunting and formidable. Yet with the best of intentions, the journey is far more rewarding than if we move toward it with harbored anxiety about outcomes. Your expectations may be high, but remember there is no single "right way" to explore one's self. Your approach will be as idiosyncratic as you are, and possibly very different from one day or week to the next.

Over time you will not simply *be* in the realm of silence and solitude, but find yourself in some way *remade* by it. Try to fully inhabit these elusive states of being. The most precious gift of being quiet and alone is the chance to reach a more genuine part of ourselves, a deep place we too often are separated from by everyday din and clamor. Immersion in silence and solitude encourages us to observe our restless minds and seductive emotions from a healthy and accepting perspective of grace, tenderness, and acceptance.

FIVE WAYS TO GET STARTED

- *Make a personalized "inventory" of times and places in your schedule that you feel would best accommodate an ongoing embrace of silence and solitude.*

- *Mark "quiet alone-time" on your calendar, the same way you would note a business appointment or a trip to the dentist. This will give these moments the respect they deserve.*

- *Notice how you respond—emotionally, physically, psychologically— when your life feels overcrowded, out of control, or excessively noisy. At the same time, pay attention to your feelings when moments of silence and solitude come along. Ask yourself, "What can I learn from these experiences?"*

- *When you inhabit quiet alone-time, turn off the phone, lock the door, ignore your e-mail, and resist the temptation to read or listen to music. Instead, disconnect from all extraneous "input" so that you may find stillness within.*

- *Talk to those closest to you—your spouse, partner, children, parents, siblings, best friend—about the ways you and they relate to silence and solitude, to noise and congestion, to distractions and overloads. Feel free to express whatever concerns each of you may have about carving out time for yourselves to be quiet and alone.*

- *Learn more about the gifts of silence and solitude, drawing on some of the resources listed in the back of this book. Ask yourself why you are interested in this topic, and let your truthful response help guide your exploration.*

After more than three months of being quiet and alone, I welcomed being busy and relished socializing again. Yet I realized I also missed the silence and solitude I had enjoyed. I had come to depend on the "wide margins" of my life, to borrow Thoreau's phrase, as a place to get my bearings and find my balance. As much as I enjoyed interacting with *others*, I wanted space in which I could interact with *myself*.

When I did find intervals of downtime, being alone for an hour or two felt wonderful: luxurious, healing, calming, and exhilarating. I both needed and wanted to make a new habit out of creating these oasislike islands of serenity. The pertinent question was, "How?" The answer sounded simple: "Figure out a way to disconnect from distractions and set an appointment with myself to be quiet and alone." But, as we all know, the simplest goals are often the most difficult to achieve.

"You need to start slowly, with baby steps," advised a friend, whose long-time experience as a teacher had rendered many truths about how people learn. "If you take on too much," Karen said, "you are likely to feel overwhelmed and discouraged. Set a realistic target of settling down for about fifteen minutes each day. Once you've made this a habit, you can try making your island of calm a little bigger."

I did as Karen suggested, and I discovered that disconnecting from my overbooked life was not so difficult after all. And because my experiences with silence and solitude felt so rewarding, I rarely felt I was giving up anything of greater importance.

SEPT. 8—138 DAYS AFTER MY RETURN

I have broken a cycle of rote behavior. My weekday mornings used to follow a clockwork pattern. I'd invariably wake up, listen to the NPR news while lying in bed, take a shower, and then prepare and drink a caffe latte while reading a magazine or newspaper. This went on for years, and I felt content.

Somehow, over the past four months, I've concluded I'm not missing anything by ignoring the news first thing in the morning. There was always a report that agitated or outraged me, often putting me in a foul mood. If I wanted to learn the news of the day, it could come later. The caffeine didn't help either. I've given up coffee altogether for tea.

I've replaced old rituals with new ones. I often sit in the morning sun with my eyes closed, meditating on my slow breath or the sounds of birds flitting nearby. I stretch and let my body awaken. I listen to soft music or play my flute. If the weather is nice, I walk in the garden with my tea and admire the plants. It's amazing how much I see, with greater clarity and detail than before. I'm almost always in a good mood now when my "work day" begins, unlike a year ago, when I often felt agitated.

Although it may not seem possible on first glance, it is likely that you already have enough discretionary time and space to bring at least ten or fifteen minutes of silence and solitude into your daily life. When I first adopted this ritual, the time was there when I needed it.

Most of us will find such opportunities in the margins of our lives, during the unstructured moments between appointments and obligations. Examine your day and you should find at least a few loose ends. For example, most of us have idle moments when we may feel an urge to flick on the TV, call a friend, munch on a snack, or get lost in a paperback. For some of us, choosing to be silent and solitary—instead of yielding to such tempting distractions—will be enough to get a healthy new habit started.

TIMES AND PLACES TO NURTURE SILENCE AND SOLITUDE

Although we may feel like we have no real say about how we spend our time, a careful and honest examination reveals this cannot literally be true. We make choices each day that explicitly reflect our personal values and individual priorities. When these commitments shift, so can our decisions about how we use our discretionary time and space.

Here are some times and places to consider for your adoption of quiet alone-time:

- *Right after you get up in the morning. You may wish to wake up a bit earlier in order to accommodate this alone-time.*

- *During moments you would otherwise spend watching mediocre or negatively themed TV shows.*

- *Commuting or running errands in your car. Turn off the music or radio and enjoy your own thoughts and perceptions.*

- *In your bedroom: create a "retreat space."*

- *As part of a soothing hot bath. Make it more luxurious with salts, scents, or candles. If you have no bathtub, make an appointment to visit a spa, hot springs, upscale hotel, bed-and-breakfast, or friend's hot tub.*

- *While sitting in a waiting room, a doctor's office, or a dentist's chair.*

- *As part of scheduled breaks at work or, if you're a student, between classes.*

- *In your spare (or guest) room, which might become a destination for mini-retreats.*

- *In an unused office or employee lounge at work or in school, perhaps used by others for this purpose.*

- *In your own garden, yard, or a nearby public park.*

- *In a local church, temple, mosque, or shrine, including surrounding gardens.*
- *During a walk. Remember that motion keeps the left side of the brain busy, while the right side is free to wander, uncensored and imaginative.*

As you make shifts in the way you use your time, you will confront resistance—from yourself and others. Friends and family may not understand why you are doing things differently, even when you explain your reasons. Within yourself, the part of you that dislikes change and craves predictability will put up a fight. These struggles are instructive in themselves, because they reveal how attached we are to what is predictable, even when the familiar no longer serves us.

My first week at the wilderness ranch was the toughest of the fourteen I spent there. Like a pet that automatically checks its food bowl to see if any goodies have appeared during even the shortest absence, I found my brain giving strong signals at predictable intervals. "Let's dash out the front door and pick up today's newspaper," an unseen voice told me, and I would step into a snowdrift that covered the front porch. "I wonder if I have any new e-mail messages," that same voice would dictate, oblivious to my lack of a computer connection. Late each morning, the internal robot would announce: "The letter carrier must have come by now; let me see what was delivered."

I was startled at the realization that much of my "normal" daily life was given over to automatic behaviors. My habituated mind was still trying to rule me. Like a hamster on a treadmill, I was trapped by my own petty routines, from my first-thing-out-of-bed coffee to bookreading before light's out. Although I saw no need to judge any of these habits as good or bad—they seemed rather benign—I could not help but interpret them as an impediment to creative thinking. Was I content? Was something important missing from my life? Were some of my routines bringing me no real pleasure? I would never know the answers to such questions as long as I distanced myself from them through disconnected motion, which I might have continued for years had it not been for this deliberate interruption.

JANUARY 19—DAY 1

Things I notice so far: the silence feels like wads of cotton in my ears all the time. It is thrilling and intimidating to decide what to do, hour by hour, which is something I am not used to. The quiet is a mirror held up to my brain reflecting—with awful certainty—things my mind does that aren't entirely flattering.

JANUARY 20—DAY 2

My only big concern is that I may be taking on too much. I worry that I might be keeping my head so busy that there will not be enough room to engage my spirit and heart, not to mention my body. As always, I must learn to focus and balance—a lifelong lesson. With all this time on my hands, the responsibility for the balancing act lies squarely on my shoulders. I see how easy it is in "real" life to blame others and to play the victim, but that doesn't cut it when one is alone and isolated.

One of the most remarkable aspects of abiding in solitude is the discovery that, with our detached, directed attention, we can actually *use* our mind to *watch* our mind. This distinctly human ability allows us to stand aside and study our own mental processes (including psychological gameplaying) at work.

Meditation teacher and *Inquiring Mind* magazine columnist Wes Nisker writes that some of his first-level students are shocked when they see "how sensations, perceptions, emotions, thinking, and consciousness all arise and interact with each other." During silent observation we discover that our brain usually is content to proceed on automatic pilot, responding to its perceptions of reality with no apparent oversight. The recognition that our mind has a mind of its own, as it were, can itself be liberating. As a wise friend of mine once put it, "To see the mind is to free the mind." Phrased another way, "seeing is relieving."

Despite its stubborn willfulness, the mind can prove a useful ally during quiet alone-time. It helps to bring at least three discrete mental states to bear during the experience of silence and solitude: desire, motivation, and persistence. Each, in its own way, encourages us to make room for a new way of being in the world. In fact, their collective cheerleading presence seems to facilitate learning and personal transformation in any context.

The first element is *desire*, a wish to inhabit the silence and solitude with as much neutral, nongrasping awareness as possible. Second is *motivation*, a willingness to commit to our own quiet alone-time for whatever gifts and insights it may bring to us. The third ingredient is *persistence*, a determination to continue steadily in a course of action that brings intentional moments of silence and solitude into our lives.

Why are these factors so important? Without desire and its cousin, motivation, you and I would never change. Desire and motivation drive our behavior. We are hardwired to react to various stimuli on the basis of cravings and aversions. Sophisticated advertising, promotion, and marketing campaigns constantly stimulate our biological and psychological urges, seeking to motivate us to behave in a particular way: buying, voting, listening, selling, watching, and so on. The underlying message is that we will gain some kind of reward—ranging from physical pleasure to more effective government—if we respond in a certain way.

Because many elements of modern American society encourage us to make our lives "better," many of us seek new ways of *being* in the world. We feel motivated to explore, play, and experiment as well as to buy new products or services. An innate curiosity and a compelling eagerness to take chances—at least low-risk ones that show reasonable odds of improving life—are part of the American character. If nothing else, we are a nation that has great faith in the reinvention of self.

MARCH 29—DAY 70

Today was the first day I had no working batteries for my radio. I like to listen to a classical music program on Sunday morning, but today I had to switch to my tape player, which still has some juice. I can see how I've developed new habits here, just as I had routines at home. I may feel like I'm being spontaneous and experimental, but after more than two months alone, I've created cozy familiarity again!

The difference is that it's easier to give up particular habits now. I'm not so attached to the notion that things should be a certain way. After a day or two, I will adjust to not having a radio.

Solitude provides a context in which we can settle into meditation and reflection. There is a place within our culture's celebration of self-discovery for being quiet, alone, and still. Most of us, even extroverts, are motivated to seek silence and alone-time once in a while, if only to unwind and decompress. Why? In part because the vast majority of adults spend a large percentage of their time working, and, as writer Barbara Holland points out in *One's Company*, "jobs heavy on human contact leave us content to be alone." Holland relates the story of her one-time neighbor, Eileen, a physical therapist: "All day there were hands snatching at her, reaching out for help, and demands on her sympathy and attention. I asked her if she minded eating alone every night and she laughed incredulously." At dinnertime "she sat down alone, in the cool of solitude, and let her spirit come trickling back to her."

Once our psyches are engaged by desire and motivation, our actions must be appropriate if we are to achieve our goals. Through the third key element of persistence, perhaps with outside support, we actualize our desires. In my experience, it is not enough simply to want quiet alone-time; I need to *honor* this state of being and *invite* it into my life.

To incorporate any new ritual into our daily routine, we need to make room for it. We have to fight the inertia and dominance of old routines and habits. It is always tempting to take the easy way out, particularly when extenuating circumstances (like illness, work deadlines, or travel) arise. But behavioral psychologists report that if we do not persist at a new habit for at least two months, it is unlikely to take root.

Thus, we must commit to running our own lives, rather than allowing our lives to run us. When we take the critical first step of deciding what we want to be different, the process of profound change begins. Sometimes when this occurs, our unconscious or intuitive mind reveals the truth about our lives in unexpected ways, as if guided by an unseen hand. "A whole stream of events issues from the decision [to commit to change]," the eighteenth-century German poet Johann Wolfgang von Goethe wrote in his *Criticisms, Reflections, and Maxims.* This raises "in one's favor all manner of unforeseen incidents and meetings and material assistance, which no man could have dreamed would have come his way. . . . Boldness has genius, power, and magic in it."

There is no "right" or "wrong" time or place to inhabit silence and solitude, which is why it is helpful to remain flexible, even in defining those terms. For me, time spent in the serenity of nature is always calming and balancing. Even a short walk in a city park does wonders for my psyche. Indoors, I set aside part of my spare room to experience silence and solitude. This is the same room I use for yoga exercise, reading spiritual books, and meditation. Such "sacred spaces" may include a small altar or the display of objects that hold special meaning. Other quiet places I enjoy include a local Zen Buddhist center and, particularly, my old-fashioned bathtub. The latter is soothing on a cold night, when steam, scented bath oil, and candles create a comforting ambiance.

An office represents a different kind of challenge—although I remember spending some very satisfying alone-time enjoying the roof-top garden of a high-rise building I worked in. Currently, I have a sepa-

CREATING A PERSONAL REFUGE IN YOUR HOME

Any place we live must accommodate a number of activities: socializing, sleeping, cooking, eating, bathing, relaxing. But what about quiet alone-time? Renowned mythologist Joseph Campbell insisted we all need a place to "simply experience and bring forth what [we] are and what [we] might be." If it doesn't already exist in your home, consider creating a kind of sanctuary (or sanctuaries) where you and other family members can go to experience silence and solitude. This space will be welcoming as a function of its serenity, beauty, and privacy. Suggestions include:

• A corner of a bedroom or spare room works well. Most of us don't have space enough to devote an entire room to such a refuge, and there is no particular need to do so.

• Place yourself beyond the sounds of TV, radio, electronic games, music players, and so on.

• Get rid of background noise, which is distracting when we seek quiet.

• Minimize clutter. Having too much "stuff" around is another kind of distraction, which can drain our energy and undermine our internal reflection.

• Make the area aesthetically pleasing. Plants or flowers tend to promote a sense of peacefulness, as do favorite beautiful objects, photographs, or paintings. Positive associations may arise from pictures of loved ones (including pets), past and present.

• Leave work somewhere else. Any reminders of obligations beyond your retreat space may make it more difficult to settle your mind and rest your spirit.

• Sound-masking devices, ranging from white noise generators to self-contained fountains, may make it easier to forget what is going on in the clamorous world beyond your home. Soft, soothing music is another option.

• Consider using your space for other mind-body activities that are potentially stress reducing or sacred to you, such as yoga, meditation, prayer, and chanting.

rate work space with a small altar, a window looking onto my rosebushes, and a carpeted area suitable for yoga, meditation, and contemplative sitting. When I travel, I look for accommodations that offer some space to abide quietly.

After we connect with silence and solitude, the workaday world gradually may begin to look and feel slightly different. This fresh perspective has the power to change our lives. For instance, we can change our relationship with *ourselves*—simply paying closer attention to how we spend our time. Some among us may begin, easily and willingly, to streamline an overcommitted lifestyle. Others may discover that *less* really is *more*, that a simpler life can be a richer and more satisfying one. The possibilities are endless. Those Saturdays of childhood can live within us once again, if only for a few minutes each morning.

BENEFITS OF SILENCE AND SOLITUDE

While great attention is devoted to the perceived *negative* aspects of being alone, surprisingly little has been written about the *positive* attributes of silence and solitude. Our most celebrated thinkers and pundits tend to reflect the prevailing view that humans are social, gregarious, and crowd-loving animals by nature. Many insist that a desire to separate from the group is somehow a dysfunctional or even a hostile act. A growing number of commentators, however, offer alternate interpretations of human needs, desires, and behaviors (see Recommeded Sources: Specific Benefits of Silence and Solitude). Here are some of the most frequently observed associations with quiet alone-time. What would you add to this list?

- Freedom to fantasize.
- Development of the imagination.
- Cultivation of abstract thought.
- Heightened awareness.
- Healing during stress, mourning, or other trauma.
- Improved concentration.
- Access to religious, spiritual, or mystical experiences.
- Better problem-solving abilities.
- Liberation from unwanted distractions.
- Effective pain management skills.
- The rich company of one's mind, body, and spirit.
- Expanded self-understanding.

CHAPTER FOUR

THE SILENT HABIT

You cannot pay attention to silence without
simultaneously becoming still within: silence
without, stillness within.

—Eckhart Tolle, *The Power of Now*

A while back I took out a loan and had fancy new windows installed in my fifty-year-old house. The ancient, badly warped windows had single-pane glass and leaked a lot of air. During winter, the cold crept in and my rooms felt drafty. I was delighted when my heating bill dropped by half after the insulated double-panes were installed.

But that's not all.

My house became surprisingly quiet. Suddenly—and unexpectedly—I realized how much noise I'd put up with during the previous ten years, even though my city is small and nonindustrial.

Gone was the hum of traffic, the wail of sirens, and the insistent beep of trucks backing up. I no longer heard my neighbors' barking dogs, the repetitive whistle of an unseen cockatoo, or the drummer two doors down the street. I didn't have to listen to the recess bells of the nearby elementary school or the chimes of the church around the corner. I was only dimly aware of airplanes and helicopters flying overhead. I could ignore the booming speakers of the teenagers who cruised my street on weekends. The droning air conditioners of summer were gone.

A more tranquil environment helped me rest at the end of a hard day. I slept better. My blood pressure and pulse rates dropped. I breathed more deeply, slowly, and fully. When I wrote in my studio, I found it easier to concentrate and to become absorbed in tasks at hand. When friends and family members came to visit, they didn't have to vie for my attention with unbidden tumult from the outside world.

Of course, getting away from the planet's ambient noise is not as simple as installing soundproof windows and keeping them closed (although that's not a bad start). On today's Earth, true silence—and the peace it affords—is hard to find, and getting harder. In the twenty-first century, quiet places are most notable by their absence. Noises and intrusions—many of them having to do with various forms of making, moving, buying, and selling products—seep into every nook and cranny, invading even our most personal spaces. I have bought gasoline and been pitched products over video screens, unseen speakers, and the pump itself. I have discharged my bodily functions in restrooms where merchandise is promoted on walls and mirrors—even *inside* toilets and urinals.

In every inhabited corner of the world, it seems, a Tower of Babel blares. The presence of artificial sounds and unwanted advertising is nearly inescapable. Aural clutter confronts us through mass media messages, public address systems, electronic hums, motorized vehicles, amplified music, and the dull background drone of generic activity.

The steady erosion of public silence is confirmed by the experience of Gordon Hempton, a professional sound recordist who since 1981 has compiled an expanding archive of Earth's natural soundscapes. Hempton, who lives in the coastal Washington city of Port Angeles, uses sophisticated tape recorders and sensitive microphones to preserve the pristine resonance of rain forests, mountain streams, ocean coastlines, prairie meadows, and other sound-rich environments.

In 1998, while I lay beneath a blanket of silence in New Mexico's northern mountains, Hempton toured fifteen states in a quest for secluded outdoor locations that one might expect to be free of human-made noise. He was surprised to find only two areas—isolated parts of the Colorado Rockies and Minnesota's Boundary Waters—that were free of motors, airplanes, and gunshots for more than fifteen minutes during daylight hours. In the March 1999 issue of *Cooking Light* magazine, Hempton said that even in remote parts of Montana and the Dakotas "it was difficult to find a noise-free interval that exceeded a minute and a half." Back in Washington, the recordist revisited twenty-one sites where he had recorded silent sequences of fifteen minutes or more back in 1984. Only three remained in 1998.

One surprising aspect of Hempton's ongoing odyssey has been his discovery that, no matter where he goes, many residents either take no notice of local background noise or are so inured to it that they don't believe it exists. If you count yourself among the latter, Hempton insists that either "you aren't really listening or you have a hearing impairment." The ambient sound is there but has become so pervasive that we accept its ubiquitous presence as "normal."

We are fooling ourselves if we believe a constant backdrop of unnatural sound does not affect us adversely. Many scientific studies confirm that while we may develop the ability to screen unwanted background noise out of our higher levels of consciousness—as a necessary adaptation for survival—the stuff nonetheless has a negative impact on our physical and mental well-being. Unfortunately, short of earplugs, there are few effective ways to shut out much of the extraneous sounds that bombard us in public places.

Those who study the impact of sound on people recognize the

negative effects of living in a noise-saturated world. "When our ears are receiving too much information, we become insecure and stressed," recordist Hempton observed during an interview with the Public Broadcasting Service. "When we're in a quiet place, like a church, concert hall, or library, we feel more relaxed." As we notice these cause-and-effect reactions in our own lives, intervals of silence often become more appealing.

Based on my wilderness foray, the observations of Hempton and other experts ring true. After ten days in a relatively mute alpine landscape, the tensions I had stored in my body and mind began melting away. As a result, my entire outlook began to shift, as reflected in my journal entries:

HOW TELEVISION DISPLACES SILENCE AND SOLITUDE

Television—the antithesis of natural sound—is a marvelous invention that can enlighten, inform, and entertain. When used judiciously, it is a delightful companion and important eye on the world. But there are aspects to the medium that pose a constant threat to quiet alone-time.

Even though various forms of TV have, without debate or consent, invaded such public spaces as airports, airplane cabins, supermarkets, and waiting rooms, this universal medium is still one of the distractions we have the most control over once we get inside our own homes. Simply turning it off—or at least becoming more selective in the programs we watch—can provide many of us with an extra twenty discretionary (and potentially noise-free) hours each week. For millions of people, this may be the easiest place to claim a little silence and solitude each day. Simply dropping one daily sitcom or newscast from our TV diet could provide an instant opportunity to adopt this ritual. When you turn off the tube, consider the following statistics:

- According to the A.C. Nielsen Company, by the middle of 2002, the average American watched nearly four hours of TV each day, seven days a week, or the equivalent of about fifty-seven days of nonstop TV viewing annually. This represented roughly 40 percent of their available leisure time.

- In its January 2000 newsletter, the Center for the New American Dream reported the Kaiser Family Foundation's finding that 49 percent of Americans under the age of eighteen live in homes where there are no rules about watching TV.

JANUARY 22—DAY 4

My day has fallen into a set of responses based largely on circumstance rather than a mindless routine or a deliberate schedule. I am not guided by the hubbub of an urban day, with its bracketing rush hours and noon whistles, but more by the interplay of light and dark, chill and warmth, sun and moon.

JANUARY 25—DAY 7

The sun drops behind the western ridge at about 4:15, but it is light for another ninety minutes. Even at 6 P.M. there is a faint glow in the west. I find myself staring in absolute awe at a sunset that seems to change in color and shadow with each passing second. As I do this, the only sign that there is an "outside world" beyond the confines of this wilderness are the high-altitude contrails that form straight lines across the top of the sky, tracing airline routes between Los Angeles, San Diego, or Phoenix and the cities to my east.

I discarded old habits during my first week alone. New reflexes grew out of the softer, calmer environment of silence and solitude. I became sensitized to everything around me, as the winter landscape presented itself fresh and glistening each morning. Mundane tasks like brushing my teeth became heightened sensually, as if I was feeling for the first time the stimulating texture of bristles against my gums and the minty taste of toothpaste on my tongue. As internal spaces previously filled by the myriad distractions of daily life presented themselves, I replenished them with an expanding awareness of the moment-by-moment adventure of being fully alive.

JANUARY 24—DAY 6

I skied to the ranch's entrance gate. Saw a bobcat track just past the cabin. The cat had followed my tracks from yesterday, so its spoor was less than eighteen hours old. I also found fresh elk tracks, some near the upper meadow and a lone set in the aspen. Nature holds me in its thrall. I am strangely, indescribably happy.

When I returned from my sojourn in nature, I discovered I was not alone in noticing the calming effect of a noise-free environment. In conversations with friends, I was astonished to learn that many were active (and often secret) seekers of silence and solitude, even though they lived in cities. These friends said that shutting off some potential source of discord—as in driving a car without music playing or spending an evening without phone calls or mass media—helped them feel serene and balanced.

"I have learned that sometimes even talking with my husband, Paul, can feel like just another distraction," Suzanne told me. "I've discovered that I can simply be silent with him, and he with me. We both find that incorporating occasional solitude during normal daily activities often leads to willingly letting go of what we call 'busy behaviors.'"

Since I first spoke with them about this topic, Suzanne and Paul have instituted sporadic "technology-free weekends," during which they consciously avoid TV, radio, computers, or recorded music. "We still use the refrigerator, stove, and other appliances," Suzanne emphasizes. "We're not total Luddites; but freeing ourselves from the other stuff once in a while has proven very liberating."

A parallel experience is recounted in Stephen Levine's *Planet Steward,* a journal describing his year-long experience as a resident caretaker for a southern Arizona nature preserve. With spouse and infant daughter, Levine relocated to this wildlife sanctuary from San Francisco, where he had led an overstimulated life as a trend-setting newspaper editor. Within their first month in Arizona, Levine noticed a profound change in his and his wife Patricia's outlook: "As we become still, things seem to come closer to the continuum. . . . Waking each morning less scrambled than the day before . . . passing from moment to moment. . . . There is a daily reorientation to a desire for peace."

I equate this to the settling that occurs in a pond as its surface shifts from turbulence to stillness. Agitation, froth, and suspended particles make it impossible to see clearly to the bottom. Whatever lies below remains invisible until the water is becalmed. Similarly, it is difficult to see what the mind contains when it is too stirred by distractions. Remove these impediments and the mind stills, allowing an encounter with whatever lies at its depths.

One of the most useful outcomes of inhabiting quiet alone-time is that it helps us develop a kind of clear seeing, an ability to ascertain fundamental truths about our lives—truths that tend to get hidden by the busyness that often overwhelms us. With this clarity we can set realistic priorities each hour, each moment. Since we have only a finite amount of time—and there are an infinite number of things we *could* do and may very well *want* to do in that time—there is no alternative to making difficult choices. Indeed, on some basic level, this is what life is about: living involves always choosing one activity over another.

When we seek quiet alone-time we are reasserting our instinctive and intuitive wisdom. We respond to a part of us that "knows" how to meet our own needs. We show kindness and compassion not only to ourselves, but to everyone around us.

Clear-seeing helps us make lists of things we want or need to do in a given day and to prioritize them. We need to stay flexible enough to throw out certain items—or possibly our entire "to do" list—if unexpected obligations come up. With newfound focus, it is easier to see what our priority should be for the next hour, the following hour, and so forth. We become less likely to feel inundated or out of control. Over time, we may also discover the rhythm of life that is most conducive to our well-being, rather than trying to adapt to a momentum set by others.

FINDING YOUR NATURAL PACE

In A Still Forest Pool, *Jack Kornfield and Paul Breiter quote one of Thailand's foremost spiritual leaders, Achaan Chaa, who has said that each person has a "natural pace" that is unique to that individual. It may be faster or slower as compared to others. Through the experience of silence and solitude, we may learn what our natural pace is and how to manifest it in daily life. The idea is to find your own momentum and try to stick with it, regardless of how fast (or slowly) those around you seem to be moving. Here are some techniques for finding your stride:*

- *Pay attention to your breathing in various situations. If it is rapid, forced, shallow, or irregular, you are probably going too fast. If it is even, slow, and deep, the pace may be just right. If the rate is so languid that you get sleepy, things are likely going too slow.*

- *Try doing things faster or slower than you usually do them. This includes walking, speaking, or working. Notice how you feel in different modes. When you return to your "normal" pace, ask yourself what feels most appropriate for you.*

- *Take a break and walk outdoors. Watch the speed of things you observe: cars on the road, trees waving in the breeze, traffic lights changing, birds flying, and so on. When you go inside, reflect on how you responded to the rates of movement you saw.*

• *Notice the relationship between your productivity, your happiness, and the speed of your life as it relates to them. We tend to be most productive and most happy when we are operating at a rhythm that suits us: our natural pace.*

From the teachings of Achaan Chaa as
disseminated by Suzanne Kryder, Inc.

One simple and effective strategy for ritualizing silence and solitude is changing how we think about these states of being. When we come to regard quiet alone-time as a needed respite from the cares and woes of daily life, we make take it more seriously. If we agree that constant stress is bad for us, as doctors and other health professionals will attest, we may feel more justified (and less guilty) in deciding to step away from the sources of such tension for at least a few minutes each day.

Many people I know deliberately set aside about thirty minutes each day to enjoy quiet alone-time, an amount others may need to build up to over months. Some individuals may withdraw from unwanted noise and activity simply by puttering in a garden, sitting in an easy chair, or resting on a couch at home. Thousands of people also take a week or two off every year to engage in a deliberate slowing down of their lives through a meditation retreat, an easygoing family vacation, or extended time spent in nature.

Such "tending to ourselves" builds on a venerable tradition that crosses all human boundaries of race, geography, creed, income, and lifestyle. Indeed, the practice of personal retreat as a source of healing and renewal may have been around as long as members of our species have walked upright.

In his book, *Hermits: The Insights of Solitude,* contemporary historian Peter France says that the Taoist philosophers of ancient China believed silence and solitude were healthy because they remove us from "the mutilating pressures of society and expose us to the healing influence of nature. We are part of the natural world and should allow our personalities to be shaped by natural forces." Chuang Tzu, a Taoist philosopher who lived about 350 B.C., quotes Confucius: "Men do not mirror themselves in running water, they mirror themselves in still water. Only what is still can still the stillness of other things."

For at least three thousand years, spiritual teachers of East and West have encouraged the use of quiet alone-time as a path to self-inquiry, restoration, and wisdom. Practicing prayer, meditation, chanting, yoga, and observation of nature are only a few of the age-old contemplative activities that link body, mind, heart, and spirit. For generations people have practiced these techniques—alone or in groups—and as a result experienced more focused concentration, reduced stress, manageable pain, healthful rejuvenation, and expanded awareness. This is not to say that *every* practitioner has encountered these results or even sought them. Certainly, many devotees have followed the rituals of their faith primarily for religious reasons, such as honoring God or seeking enlightenment. It is not my intention to dismiss or diminish religious motivations for contemplative activity, but merely to note the potential of prayers, chants, yoga, immersion in nature, and withdrawal to solitude to exert a wide-ranging influence on any individual, even in ancient times.

Among the ancient Greeks, the search for the meaning of life was carried out in solitude at least as often as it was in debate and discussion. The expectation was that obtaining valuable insights required deliberate effort and reflection. "In searching out the truth," the Athenian philosopher Heraclitus wrote, "be ready for the unexpected. For it is difficult to find and puzzling when you find it."

Among the world's major religions, the monastic lifestyle is praised, accommodated, and revered. Jesus Christ, Moses, Mohammed, Confucius, Lao Tzu (the founder of Taoism), and Prince Siddhartha (the Buddha) sequestered themselves for hours, weeks, months, and sometimes years in order, among other goals, to sort out their thoughts and emotions, as have thousands of lesser-known seekers. It is a mistake to assume these individuals renounced the company of others simply because they had an aversion to people or sought to escape an oppressive reality. In a place of abiding peace, free of distraction, such solitaries could study and understand themselves—as well as others—more fully. When they returned to the "real" world, many of these individuals offered their insight, love, and compassion as gifts. In incalculable ways, the fruits of their quiet lives have helped reorder priorities and redefine values for the rest of us. When we taste a bit of this, new possibilities may present themselves, and even seem more achievable.

"I must not go into solitude to immobilize my life, to reduce all things to a frozen concentration upon some inner experience," the Trappist monk and occasional hermit Thomas Merton wrote in his personal journal. "In solitude I become fully able to value what I cannot know."

WHAT WOULD YOU DO IF YOU HAD MORE FREE TIME?

If we were liberated from pressing obligations, such as earning a living or raising children, most of us could name a hundred things we would like to do. Here's my own short list:

- *Write a novel.*
- *Visit family members.*
- *Get reacquainted with old friends.*
- *Ski in the backcountry.*
- *Organize personal photographs.*
- *Tour Italy.*
- *Learn to play a musical instrument.*

Why is it, then, that few of us find—or make—the time to follow our heart's desire? The incessant activity of our lives distances us, to some degree, from our longings. Because we cannot fully feel, touch, or even know such dreams, we do not pursue them.

Help yourself create a new reality. Make a list of things—from the magnificent to the ordinary—that you would like to do or experience if only you had more free time. It may be as simple as refinishing a favorite old chair or taking a child on a camping trip, as ambitious as losing ten pounds or becoming fluent in Spanish. If you do not believe you have time even to write such a list, think again. The simple boldness of describing these aspirations invests them with power, frequently enough to actualize them. Consider using your personal journal as a repository for such a free-spirited list.

When we embark on an inner journey we often seek to understand the origins of delusional or clouded thinking and blocked or fuzzy emotions. This, in turn, may help us change our relationship to the underlying sources of these thoughts and feelings. For some of us, revelations and connections—powerful enough to change fundamental perspectives on life—may occur when we break our routines and see the world in a new way.

Several years ago, I heard the following story from a friend. He described a thirty-five-year-old New York investment banker who took a vacation in a small coastal Mexican village. One afternoon the banker stood at the end of a rickety pier. He looked out to sea and idly watched a lone fisherman in a small boat bring his catch in. The fisherman, who was about the same age as the American, began unloading several large yellow-fin tuna.

"How long did it take you to catch them?" the *gringo* wanted to know.

"Only a little while," the Mexican replied, in heavily accented English.

The banker asked why the fisherman didn't stay out longer and catch more fish.

"I take enough to support me and my family," the man shrugged.

"But what do you do with the rest of your time?"

"I sleep late in the morning before I go fishing," he explained. "After I come home, I play with my children, eat something, take a *siesta* with my wife, maybe go out and fish some more, and after dinner stroll to the plaza where I have a drink and play guitar with my *amigos*." The Mexican paused and smiled. "I have a full and busy life."

The banker scoffed. "I have an MBA from Harvard and I could help you. If you spent more time fishing you could earn enough money to buy a bigger boat that would help you catch even more fish. With such volume, you could sell your catch directly to the processor and eventually save enough to open your own cannery. That would give you control over product, processing, and distribution. With your profits you would some day be able to leave this village and buy a big house on a hill overlooking Mexico City, where you could set up a headquarters for your expanding enterprises."

The fisherman stared at the American and tugged at an earlobe. He looked the gringo in the eye and asked, "How long would all this take?"

"Maybe fifteen to twenty years."

"And what then?"

The American laughed. "That's the best part," he exclaimed. "When the time is right you can sell your company to one of your competitors and become very rich. You'd make millions!"

The fisherman's eyes twinkled. "*Sí, señor.* And after I retire I could move to a sleepy village on the coast where I would sleep late, fish a little, play with my grandchildren, take a siesta with my wife, and in the evening sip a drink while I play guitar with my amigos."

Try setting aside a few moments each day that belong not to spouse, lover, boss, kids, friends, or teachers—but simply and exclusively to you as an individual. Try starting with a brief, deliberate pause for private self-nurturing each morning, before your "public day" begins. Sit quietly and mindfully, without the usual entrapments of cooking, eating, dressing, grooming, reading, getting absorbed in the news, or interacting with others. Close your eyes and draw your attention to a place where inner sounds and voices are expressed but seldom heeded. It is in this contemplative silence and healing solitude that our deepest yearnings can be acknowledged and our most heartfelt passions touched.

NOTING THE DIFFERENCES

Without judgment or knee-jerk reaction, notice the difference in how you feel and respond during periods in which you are embracing some amount of ritualized silence and solitude versus times when you are not. Here are some relevant questions to ask yourself, none of which have a specific "correct" answer:

- *Am I responding automatically or attentively?*

- *Either way, what are the consequences of those responses?*

- *What triggers my rote behavior?*

- *How are my body's sensations and posture influenced by quiet alonetime?*

- *Do my levels of stress or anxiety change?*

- *Are my relationships with people affected?*

- *Do my feelings about the importance of taking time out vary depending on whether I consider myself busy, unhappy, relaxed, pushed, and so on?*

- *Do I like myself better—and do others like me better—when I embrace silence and solitude regularly?*

Each of us reacts to silence and solitude differently. While you may respond positively to some of the above questions, other replies may be mixed, neutral, or even negative. Essential to our understanding of these differences is that the qualities inherent within silence and solitude are themselves without any particular value. They require our attentive experience and commitment of energy to invest them with meaning, positive or negative. Our response will depend on what we bring to the still, secluded places we choose to visit inside ourselves.

Your silence and solitude can become, as the German writer Rainer Maria Rilke put it, "a hold and home for you" in an ongoing quest for understanding and inspiration. "The natural growth of your inner life will lead you slowly and with time to other insights," wrote Rilke in

Letters to a Young Poet. "Leave to your opinions their own quiet, undisturbed development, which, like all progress, must come from deep within and cannot be pressed or hurried by anything. *Everything* is gestation and then bringing forth. . . . And be considerate of [those] who fear that being-alone in which you trust."

The latter observation by Rilke is particularly important. Many of us are conditioned to fear being alone or unable to communicate with others, even for a short while. Those who love and depend upon us may react with the same emotion. Yet an embrace of silence and solitude is by its very nature an exploration of this state of disconnection. In simpler times, before the so-called Information Age, we sometimes had no choice but occasionally to be out of touch with one another, even within nuclear families.

Today, thanks to mass media and digital technology, we do not have to be alone. Ever. Nor do we need to experience a noise-free existence—unless we choose otherwise. By making such choices, we not only go against the social norm, we also step out of a constantly moving stream of divergent bits of information and entertainment that otherwise carries us along like the current of a strong river.

The irony is that all of this communication cannot begin to compensate for the isolation and loneliness that many feel, even as they enjoy the privilege of never being "out of touch" with those with whom they work, live, and play. What is missing is *direct* experience: genuine, unmediated contact with what is around us. This commonly takes the form of interaction with loved ones, animals, plants, weather phenomena, and our inner sphere of feelings, thoughts, and sensations.

Within only a few days of starting my retreat, I began to feel some loneliness. I yearned for the simple pleasures of human company, like having someone with whom I could hold a casual conversation or a companion for a leisurely walk. Without anyone to share them, preparing and eating meals felt like drudgery. Even though I cooked and ate alone in the "outside" world, I realized that I always had a distraction—often a newspaper or the day's mail—to divert me from my "aloneness." By stripping down to a more naked experience of my life, I was beginning to see what truly mattered.

JANUARY 27—DAY 9

I don't often feel lonely here, but I do notice the poignant moment when I return to the house after being gone for two hours. Nothing has been moved, no note has been written, no phone messages, no e-mail, no U.S. mail. This even though I leave the house with the doors unlocked (I have no key). It's sad and eerie, as if I've been forgotten by the world; as if I don't exist.

At night, when it is calm, the silence is complete. The land feels asleep, and even those creatures that stir during the day are curled up in their burrows or hiding places. I wish there were someone here to share my excitement with if I ever am lucky enough to catch a glimpse of the Northern Lights.

Through the embrace of silence and solitude, we may enjoy the increasingly rare privilege of seeing things as they are, not as we wish them to be nor as screened by the distraction of human artifice. By making this embrace a regular, healthful ritual, we can enjoy the sense of liberation and well-being that accompanies self-knowledge and a deeper understanding of the world we live in.

CHAPTER FIVE

CULTIVATING A TRADITION OF STILLNESS

The solitary life, being silent, clears away the smokescreen of words that man has laid down between his mind and things. In solitude we remain face to face with the naked being of things.

—Thomas Merton, *Thoughts in Solitude*

In her book, *Amazing Grace: A Vocabulary of Faith*, former art teacher Kathleen Norris recalls training South Dakota elementary school children in how to be completely quiet and still, a task that puzzled and tested some of them. "It's like we're waiting for something," said one apprehensive boy. Another young student had a very different reaction, telling his teacher: "Silence reminds me to take my soul with me wherever I go."

Norris, who is also a poet and essayist, found that the older her students were, the more they preferred making noise together rather than sitting quietly by themselves. If you've spent time with teenagers, you know that quiet alone-time is an abomination to many young people. Socializing takes center stage in a hormone-drenched world where solitude has little value.

Since the Industrial Age began, the difficulty in finding or asserting quiet alone-time has been a byproduct of society's fast-changing social, economic, and political structures. The interests of many of these institutions are often ill-served—or seriously threatened—by people spending time alone in reflection and contemplation. After all, too much critical thinking can lead to a rejection of the status quo. At a young age, in partial response to overriding cultural impulses, many of us demonstrate ambivalent or decidedly negative reactions regarding silence and solitude.

Some speculate that there is a biological as well as a cultural component to a preference for socializing over being alone. In evolutionary terms, members of the species Homo sapiens and their forebears have formed strong social bonds to survive. We have spent more time relating to our environment in groups than as individuals, and our "loners" have always been more apt to suffer from predators, diseases, accidents, and mental disorders. As a result, some biologists insist, it is simply "unnatural" for humans to lead solitary lives.

Many psychologists see virtue in companionship, tending to judge our mental health in terms of a person's capacity to form successful relationships. Behavioral scientists conclude that "solitaries" are often sickly, unhappy, and relatively short-lived. The happiest and sanest men and women, according to these researchers, are those who have good marriages and enjoy smooth relations with family members, friends, and coworkers.

History documents a long, deeply embedded Western tradition of regarding the oddball who embraces silence and solitude with amusement, suspicion, or even fear. In ancient Greece, for example, there was great praise for the rights of the individual, so long as he or she did not disrupt the prevailing social order. In 399 B.C., the philosopher Socrates was put to death partly because those in power felt that he was corrupting the youth of Athens by encouraging them to think for themselves, to rebel against authoritarian ideas and despotic leaders. With Socrates out of the way, the political and military leaders of Greece were better able to control their subjects.

Centuries later, according to some historians, the golden age of Rome stressed briefly the value of the individual and free-thinker. But the tide shifted quickly with a rise in power of the Roman Catholic Church, which demanded allegiance to a central authority and unquestioned dogma. For a millennium, the pope and his associates dictated the terms of responsible behavior in the West, which left little room for independent thought or unguided self-reflection.

Catholic dominance was followed by the emergence of the eighteenth century's Age of Reason. During this epoch, conformity was praised by an intellectual aristocracy that seemed to have no faith in the capacity of people to shape their own destiny.

"Man is born for society," French philosopher Denis Diderot argued in his influential 1796 book, *La Religieuse.* "Separate him, isolate him, and his ideas will become disjointed, his character will change, a thousand ridiculous emotions will rise in his heart [and] extravagance will rise in his spirit like brambles in a wasteland." Diderot believed humans needed "greater strength of soul to resist solitude than to resist misery. Misery degrades, solitude depraves. . . . We should avoid both."

Meanwhile, England's renowned curmudgeon and author Samuel Johnson urged Britons to keep busy and mingle with others: "If solitary, be not idle. If idle, be not solitary." Johnson groused that "the solitary mortal is certainly luxurious, probably superstitious, and possibly mad."

While Diderot and Johnson were railing against individualism and inactivity, Puritan preachers and colonial leaders across the Atlantic were advising their fellow Americans to find happiness by pressing noses to grindstones. "When men are employed, they are best contented," Benjamin Franklin wrote in a 1780 letter to George Washington. "On idle days, [men] are mutinous and quarrelsome." Ever the pragmatist, Franklin also advised that "time is money."

In modern Western industrialized countries, we now enjoy such a general surfeit of money, comforts, and amusements that deliberately stopping to "do nothing" or "look inward" seems unthinkable, even ludicrous. If we "do nothing," we reject all the things we *could* be doing. The implication is that we are shunning what others have worked so hard to provide, insulting our fellow humans in the process. We are choosing bread and water over the delectable feast laid before us. Here lies a paradox: when we take time to be with ourselves in quiet alone-time—settling into a nonacquisitive stillness—we may be enriched beyond wanting and find a contentment beyond striving.

APRIL 7—DAY 78

I find myself doing more yoga and meditation during the past week, less reading and writing. I'm giving my eyes and left brain a much-deserved rest. I can read and write anywhere, at any time, but a quiet solo experience like this is rare. I want to take full advantage of it before I leave.

At this point in my wilderness journey, my mind is quiet and contemplative. It occurs to me that I've had fewer than a half-dozen conversations (besides the ones on the radio-telephone) during the past eleven weeks. When I talk to myself—which I do from time to time—my voice seems to come from a deep, hidden place: a part of me as silent and spacious as the sky overhead.

CLEAR SEEING AS AN INVITATION TO SILENCE

Sit—or, if circumstances require, stand—in a comfortable position and allow your eyes to scan your surroundings. Take in whatever your vision encounters. Notice how your mind wants to label and categorize things, to make judgments about them, or to pull your focus into a story, a plan, a fantasy, or a memory.

Without getting drawn into this desire to frame the experience, gently—but firmly—pull your attention back to simply experiencing what lies before you, here and now. You may find your absorption with past and future diminishes as you pay a kind of neutral awareness to what is happening at this moment and in this place. This detached attentiveness is the essence of the state of awareness known as "mindfulness," which is enhanced by the experience of silence and solitude. You can apply mindful focus to good advantage in any situation in any place, whether washing dishes or listening to someone talk, exercising muscles or examining emotions.

Throughout much of Western history, prevailing attitudes toward withdrawal into silence and solitude have reflected both hypocrisy and irony. Those who have lived within the confines of society have often sought advice from those who have rejected those same strictures. The outsider is presumed to see more clearly what the rest of us—perhaps blindly—are fully engaged in.

In *Hermits,* Peter France describes how some early monastics withdrew as a means "to escape the distractions of life in the village or city, and [subsequently] found that with solitude came peace, a clearer perception of the way to spiritual health and, maybe more surprisingly, an awareness of the self-deceptions of those who lived in society."

In *Amazing Grace,* Kathleen Norris reported that the sixth-century monk Dorotheus of Gaza wrote of physical withdrawal from the outside world as a matter not of "being free from [wanting] certain things to happen" but paying close attention to those wants. Over millennia, self-styled loners have built up reputations not only for heroic spirituality and lean asceticism but for their keen insights into the human condition.

American poet Robert Lax—who spent decades living alone in a small Greek village—once said that he needed to "escape distractions in order [as a hermit] to do something which is not anti-social." In an interview with Peter France recounted in *Hermits,* Lax explained this seeming contradiction between the solitary life and social responsibility: "We [humans] all need each other far too much for somebody to take off and do nothing or to do something destructive." Like solitaries before him, the expatriate discovered that his unique perspectives on life attracted a near-constant parade of discontented Greeks who sought his advice on how they should live among one another. As a result, Lax became so famous for being a hermit that he had a hard time actually being left alone.

David Budbil, a poet and essayist who wrote *Moment to Moment: Poets of a Mountain Recluse,* once confessed to being "haunted" by how a person's withdrawal from the world can be brought into accord with the need for good citizens to be engaged with the world and helping to solve its problems. He found his answer in the words of the twentieth-century Christian monk (and occasional hermit), Thomas Merton, who insisted that the person who sees "the true state of affairs" through silence and solitude can step beyond the limitations of "self" and thereby help society at large. Thus the two sides of this coin—withdrawal and engagement—are a complement to each other rather than in conflict. A fate similar to Lax's befell Merton, who was barraged with requests from would-be visitors who wanted to disrupt the monk's solitude so that he could teach them how better to live in the "outside" world.

Veneration of the recluse as activist is very old. In ancient China, for example, a distinguished and powerful T'ang dynasty official named Wang Wei spent time as a hermit, Taoist sage, poet, and painter. He was one of many prominent men of his era who sought to balance their public and private lives.

"Seclusion and public service were seen as the dark and light of the moon," notes Bill Porter in his book about this phenomenon, *Road to Heaven: Encounters with Chinese Hermits.* "Officials who never experienced tranquillity and concentration of spirit in pursuits other than fame and fortune were not esteemed in China."

In the modern era—despite historical evidence to the contrary—voluntary exile is often dismissed as whimsical escapism, neurotic eccentricity, or myopic self-absorption rather than a route to constructive and healthy reflection. There is a vague sense of weakness or deficiency associated with personal retreat, as if separating oneself from society represents an inability to stand up to the harshness of "the real world." Many interpret self-withdrawal as a hostile act of rejection, intimidation, or self-protection. For others, aloneness feels scary, lonely, unnerving, and threatening. In family-centered or privacy-deprived cultures, including many of those found in Asia, Africa, the Arctic, and Latin America, choosing to be alone may be unfathomable. Within such a context, the choice of separateness may seem to pose a serious threat to the integrity and strength of the family unit.

"In more primitive societies all over the world, nobody lives alone, and families accrete in generational layers to the toppling point," Barbara Holland points out in *One's Company.* "There are villages where people may know solitude for only a few hours or days in a lifetime. . . . The rest of their lives they sleep ears-to-heels with all their relations and apparently like it that way."

It is possible that these so-called "primitives" are more in tune with the basic needs of humanity than those of us who presume to be "civilized." Perhaps members of these long-evolved tribes feel no need for quiet alone-time because they are happy and content with the way things are, their needs fully met by their highly developed social structures.

For the millions of us immersed in the hurly-burly of modern life, however, the domain of silence and solitude is far from static. In the course of a single day, we may be thrust in and out of noisy and crowded environments many times. We constantly cope with varying levels of distraction. We can expect our relationship to quiet alone-time to change, sometimes dramatically, depending on our outlook as well as uncontrolled circumstances. Even in isolation, internal needs and desires remain in flux. This was evident as I moved more deeply into my wilderness isolation.

MARCH 4—DAY 44

A mushy, melty day. No good for skiing or snowshoeing. I did a soggy hike instead. On the way back I found a rusty old tobacco can. This is one of the only human artifacts (translation: garbage) I have found on or near the ranch. I am surprised at how little trash there is on this land, despite a hundred years of continuous habitation.

This afternoon I finished Robyn Davidson's *Tracks,* an autobiographical account of a young Australian woman's seventeen-hundred-mile solo walk across the Outback in the company of a pet dog and four camels. An amazing and inspiring tale. Her message: We all have much more power and opportunity than we ever imagine, and the hardest part of getting what we want is making the commitment to take action toward getting it.

I could relate my three months alone to some of the changes Davidson went through while alone in the desert, and to the aliveness and attention to the present that came to her as a result. One of the difficult things about being here so long is that my shifts in awareness and recommitments to change are largely interior, I cannot actualize them here. It is frustrating to have to wait another six weeks before "engaging" with others and putting these insights and proposed behaviors to the tricky test of "reality."

Silence and solitude can be uncomfortable states for many in Western society, even those of us who choose to embrace them. Quiet alone-time presents conditions where we may have to face unwelcome and unpleasant—or at least uncomfortable—truths about ourselves. When the distractions and diversions end, we are confronted with our most genuine self, raw and exposed. If who we "really are" is at odds with the person we want or expect to be, we may avoid such introspective stillness in order to spare ourselves pain, disappointment, or embarrassment. The human ego often shrinks in the bright light of truth, preferring to remain in the dark about its own reality.

I am convinced there is also a part of our psyche that craves honesty, that will fight tenaciously to know its authentic self. For many of us, the greatest joy lies in pursuing a life that rings true. Mythologist Joseph Campbell called this "following your bliss." Living otherwise demands constant surveillance, rigid control, and enormous energy. Falsity in behavior and denial of conviction creates an inner tension that can lead to other problems, including some serious and even life-threatening physical ailments. By living more truthfully, we can relax and fulfill ourselves, perhaps for the first time.

In the midst of silence, our options expand. When we do *nothing*, we stare into the potential of *everything*. This is an essential part of the strength and allure of quiet alone-time, and one of its most important purposes.

SLOW DOWN AND LISTEN

William Isaacs writes in Dialogue and the Art of Thinking Together *that to listen to what goes on at our core "is to develop an inner silence, [which is] not a familiar habit for most of us." Such listening requires "a kind of disciplined self-forgetting." We do well to cultivate techniques for processing what flows through the mind as it abides in silence. Try some of the following:*

- *Be aware of how you listen, which is generally in an unconscious mode, like a sleepwalker. For a change in perspective, try to notice your habitual reactions to what you are hearing.*

- *Notice how your thoughts stir memories, emotions, or reactions. This exercise often reveals how many of our responses are stored and habituated, not fresh and attentive.*

- *Listen without making assumptions. It is humbling to realize how much of what we think we hear is not reality but our subjective projection of what we believe we have heard.*

- *Be aware of the gaps between what you say and what you do. Each of us does this, but it is useful to recognize how often such gaps between words and action occur.*

*• Be still long enough to know what is going on beneath the chatter of
your own mind and the minds of others. This may lead to new ways of
thinking about things and to developing creative problem-solving
strategies.*

Mindfulness and relaxation are good for their own sake, as ways of
taking care of yourself. They may be practiced without the expectation
of profound insight or expanded awareness. Reducing daily stress may be
one of the most rewarding consequences of quiet alone-time. Few
among us lead lives that cannot benefit from breaks in activity and disconnection from obligation.

But can we receive the deeper, more transformative gifts of silence
and solitude in daily life while surrounded by other people, even on a
rush-hour bus or subway in the middle of a crowded city? Can compre-
hension and self-awareness expand as we find our calm center in a busy
office or noisy household? There is no reason why we cannot develop a
finely tuned presence—the cultivated, noninterpretive attentiveness that
often stems from quiet alone-time—as we drive a car, wash dishes, wait
in a crowd, or enjoy a cup of coffee at our desk.

More important than physical environment is our mental disposition
and psychological receptivity regarding quiet alone-time. It is natural to
feel trepidation about what might emerge from within us during still,
silent moments. Since each of us has a "dark side," along with personality
traits we aren't proud of, there is bound to be some fear of what we'll see
when we look at ourselves closely. Yet the *anticipation* of what lurks
beyond the mind's smoke screen is likely to be more frightening than
what actually *exists* there. In "Thoughts and Solitude," an essay from the
book of the same name, Thomas Merton suggests that in quiet alone-
time we confront a harsh reality not with terror or shame but tender
acceptance. Such realities are thereby "clothed in the friendly communion of silence, and this silence is related to love."

The word "love" is crucial in this context. Without the presence of
love—of self, of spouse or partner, of family, of friends, neighbors, and
colleagues—we would not be doing any of this. Love comes from caring.
If we do not care about self or other, we feel no motivation or desire to
better understand either.

Our deliberate fullness of attention, wrought by silence and solitude,
may reveal to us what we really love (and don't), what is truly important

to us (and what's not), what makes us ecstatic (and what bores or drives us crazy), whom we want to be with (and whom we are ready to dismiss from our lives).

It is possible that no such insights will reveal themselves—or not right away. We must not assume that an embrace of silence and solitude is of its own accord going to provide us with *any* revelation. Bringing awareness to the present moment is not the same as thinking or reflecting upon what unfolds. We are not invited *necessarily* to self-analysis or introspection. Personal changes and better understandings may indeed come—and often do—but to anticipate that they will automatically appear can undermine and distort the process of self-discovery. The key is being attentive to our experience—and our relationship to it—as we move through daily life, even when silence and solitude are absent. This lies at the core of the concept known as mindfulness.

FEBRUARY 26—DAY 39

I just read Jon Krakauer's book, *Into Thin Air*, about an ill-fated expedition of climbers heading to the top of Mount Everest. Compared to their misadventures, my complaints and inconveniences are trivial. My life is only marginally less comfortable than it would be were I at home. The main difference is that I have virtually no human contact and must occupy myself with only what is here, including me. But after six weeks of isolation, I have concluded that reality (and how I respond to it) is all a mental exercise anyway. If I can cope with the ever-changing moment, then I can cope with anything. In the most literal sense, that's all I have. That's all anyone has.

I find it helpful to recall an observation made by health educator Saki Santorelli in his book *Heal Thy Self*. The author recalls being told by an artist and calligrapher in Japan, where Santorelli once lived, that the Japanese-language character for "mindfulness" consists of two interacting figures: one representing mind, the other heart. Thus, mindfulness is translated in Japan as bringing the "heart-mind" to the present moment, with both fields of awareness observing *together*, not separately. If we consider the *mindfulness* of quiet alone-time as a marriage of intellect and soul, rather than as the preference of one way of seeing over another, we can move beyond the limiting duality that is characteristic of Western thinking patterns.

Our intention here is to use some degree of cultivated quiet and deliberate aloneness to promote healthy living. Jon Kabat-Zinn, Santorelli's colleague at the University of Massachusetts Medical School, defines this mode of attentive awareness as "wakefulness." In *Full Catastrophe Living,* Kabat-Zinn describes mindfulness as "purposely stopping all the doing in [our] lives and relaxing into the present without trying to fill it up with anything. . . . Purposely allowing body and mind to come to rest in the moment, no matter what is 'on' [our] mind or how [our] body feels." Through mindfulness, Kabat-Zinn says we are simply allowing ourselves "to be in the moment with things exactly as they are, without trying to change anything." In a word, it is about devoting *attention* to life rather than existing in a sort of reactive fog, without examining or questioning our various assumptions, reactions, attitudes, or behaviors.

CONSCIOUS EATING AS AN EXPLORATION OF SILENCE

Since most of us eat three meals each day, we have ample opportunity to practice a conscious or mindful form of eating. Sadly, in this era of fast-food restaurants, microwave snacks, and frozen entrées, many of us prepare and consume our food unconsciously: while driving, reading, watching TV, listening to the radio, scanning mail, working, engrossed in conversation, or on the phone. We may be at a computer, standing up, or even walking down the street. Our attention is everywhere, except on the taste, appearance, smell, temperature, and texture of our meal.

One way to get off this juggernaut is to sit down and eat a single kind of food, one mouthful at a time, with focused, deliberate attention. Meditation groups sometimes use raisins to practice mindful eating. Other bite-sized foods are also appropriate: nuts, cut vegetables, and fresh fruit. Ideally, have someone else select the food for you, without your knowledge, and place it directly in your mouth while your eyes are closed. In this way, you are less likely to label, anticipate, or "judge" the food before you taste it.

As with the "conscious seeing" practice described earlier in this chapter, try to fully experience the food without getting hooked into past associations and emotions. Notice any tendency to do this, as it comes up, then gently let go and move on. Simply eat, feeling free to explore the item with your tongue, palate, and teeth. Focus on all the sensations that emanate from what you hold in your mouth. Observe how your body reacts. Does it salivate, crave more, have an urge to swallow, or find

the food distasteful? After you have finished eating, notice your emotions,
physical sensations, and what is different about eating mindfully versus
the way you usually eat.

Through the process of mindful self-discovery in quiet alone-time,
we may learn some of our deepest secrets, strongest passions, fondest
wishes, worst fears, and most genuine affections. This not only gives our
lives depth, wholeness, and meaning, it also fills a reservoir of pleasure,
resilience, courage, and strength. I often feel reinvigorated and restored. A
cascade of delights, mysteries, wonderments, terrors, and longings also
may tumble from within. The possibilities wrought by such an inner
journey may prove to be a spectrum that is amusing, challenging, disturbing, calming, and delightful.

"Nondoing" may seem simple but it certainly is not easy. Opening
the door to the unconscious mind and yearning heart rarely is. The most
fortunate thing about the transformative powers of silence and solitude is
that these tools are available to each of us, no matter where we live, at any
time, and at no cost. Quiet alone-time can be as soothing as deep slumber, as illuminating as a bright idea, and as thrilling as a love affair. Silence
and solitude require no special handshake, equipment, class, degree,
license, guru, therapist, diet, pill, religion, or jargon. They are as easy to
find as a door and four walls. They provide a means, as Thoreau observed,
to "be completely true to ourselves."

I use the term "quiet alone-time" to describe what I do because it is
accurate and free of other associations. Some who are drawn to silence
and solitude view their equivalent experience as "meditation." Others are
uncomfortable with that word because its meaning is ambiguous and
often associated with Eastern religions. These "nonmeditating medita-
tors" may want to use a different label for what they do: contemplating,
emptying, floating, communing with a greater power, or zoning out. The
exact meanings of such terms are not terribly important, as long as they
reflect our participation in silence and solitude. Another idea is to use the
words that describe the more visible activity one is outwardly engaged in:
sitting, relaxing, gardening, swimming, driving, cooking, bathing, or
walking the dog. This has the added advantage of being true: when we
mindfully walk, drive, bathe, and so on, that *is* the main focus of what we
are doing.

All humans have the power to direct their attention and awareness,
yet in daily life we seldom use this ability as a tool of self-examination.

When we practice mindfulness, whether through meditation or other focusing techniques, we are directing that attention and awareness in a close observation of who we are, here and now. As the Buddha is said to have put it, the goal is to "be a light unto ourselves."

I am not suggesting that we can contemplate our troubles away, or turn a blind eye toward real problems, such as the immense suffering in the world. Exploration of self in quiet alone-time is not about escape, nor denial. The success of living in the present moment rests on our commitment to relate honestly with ourselves and with others. Instead of remaining oblivious to what "is," we come to accept ourselves completely as we are, with neither judgment nor avoidance.

CONSCIOUS WALKING AS AN EXPLORATION OF SILENCE

The simple act of walking—something we do every day without conscious thought—is another useful object of mindfulness in quiet alone-time. Try bringing your full attention to all the movements and sensations associated with walking slowly and deliberately: engaging muscles, picking one foot up, balancing briefly on the opposite foot, shifting weight forward, and stepping down with the foot that is moving. Do this silently, intentionally, and carefully. Move in a line or circle on a relatively flat service. Direct your eyes downward at a forty-five-degree angle, about six feet ahead, so that your mind does not become preoccupied with going anywhere in particular or with what is around you.

The same kind of "nondoing" that is central to other forms of conscious awareness applies here. After a few minutes, try to synchronize your breathing cycle with your walking cycle, so that your foot moves on an inhale, for example, and your weight shifts on an exhale. After twenty minutes or so, review the state of your mind and body. If you find your attention wandering as you walk, pause and take a few deep breaths before reconnecting with the present moment and starting again.

It is beyond the purpose and scope of this book to delve into the finer points of mindfulness and meditation, although I recommend exploring these subjects further. If you feel your life is enhanced by the contemplative aspects of silence and solitude, you may wish to seek out a local meditation group, where regularly-scheduled talks on the subject are combined with periods of directed sitting or walking meditation. A growing number of classes, books, and audio- and videotapes about meditation are also available. Many meditation centers throughout the world hold silent retreats—promoting the benefits of solitude and ranging in length from a few hours to a year or more. Check the resources section at the back of this book for further information.

The same "mystic East" stigma that clouds the image of meditation for some Westerners is also sometimes attached to the meditative practice of yoga, which developed in India about five thousand years ago. While its origins are connected with the Hindu religion, engagement in yoga is not necessarily a religious activity, although for many practitioners it has a spiritual dimension. The word itself is derived from a Sanskrit term for "yoke" or "union." This is widely interpreted as a reference to the interrelationship of body and mind through the mental and physical discipline that is integral to yoga. As a yoke harnesses an ox to a specific focus for the animal's body and mind, so yoga directs our awareness in a discipline that marries the physical and intellectual, and potentially the spiritual, psychological, and emotional.

Yoga involves purposefully and mindfully stretching and strengthening muscles, tissues, ligaments, and tendons with deliberate attention paid to breath, balance, and various sensations that may arise during specific postures. For most practitioners, the result is not only greater strength and flexibility, but a calming of the mind coupled with a refinement of focus on the present.

Yoga in the United States is often practiced in class settings within formats that include time limits, music, teacher instruction, use of props, and specific goals. Yet even within this context, a practitioner can move toward an inner state of silence and solitude despite the proximity of

---

YOGA IN AMERICA

According to Richard Corliss's article "The Power of Yoga" in the April 23, 2001 issue of *Time*, some form of yoga was being practiced by an estimated 15 million Americans. Three out of every four health clubs in the United States now offer some form of this exercise. As yoga has moved into the mainstream, specialized classes and workshops have become available in even small communities. Check phone directories, bulletin boards, the Internet, and listings in local publications for information about classes and teachers, most of whom have specialized training as well as extensive experience.

others and other potential distractions. In yoga, as in many other activities, mental discipline can be used to cultivate a sense of separateness or nonattachment that allows a person to enjoy stillness and tranquillity. As one becomes more proficient and confident, yoga can be practiced on one's own. No matter what the physical setting, mindful yoga in any variant of quiet alone-time exists in a "nondoing" state of acceptance of what "is," rather than a striving for what "is not."

In yoga we can make contact with the silence and solitude that we carry within us at all times. It is here that we fully "listen" to our bodies, through an awareness of balance, breath, shifting energies, and our capacities of strength and flexibility. By monitoring your feelings, thoughts, and spirits as you practice mindful yoga, you can integrate primary aspects of your being simultaneously.

Among the benefits of yoga are greater confidence in (and knowledge of) the abilities of our bodies and minds, reduced stress, a stronger immune system, and a general feeling of relaxation and well-being. Over time, you may come to know the ways your mind relates to sensations, including chronic pain, agitation, and stress, as well as fear, resistance, avoidance, detachment, and anxiety. Through regular attentive yoga practice, you can learn a great deal about healing, soothing, and balancing.

Although I had some experience with yoga prior to my wilderness retreat, I made a strong, ongoing commitment to the practice after my return. In the years since then, I have spent several hours each week doing yoga. Like other health-promoting habits, I find that yoga is its own reward. In addition to many of the specific benefits outlined above, I like how I feel when yoga is part of my life, physically and mentally.

As a long-time practitioner I can vouch for yoga's transformative power, and I suggest that you give yoga a try if you have not done so already. Like sitting in silence and solitude, it has the advantage of being free and accessible to people of almost any age, health status, body type, or physical ability. You can practice yoga in a wide variety of settings, with no or few props (a plastic mat and appropriate clothing are helpful), and it has the potential to provide enormous healing benefits over one's lifetime. One may choose from an array of yoga variants; see the resources section at the back of this book for relevant information.

Yoga and meditation are useful applications of silence and solitude in daily life, but they are far from the only vehicles for gaining insight and developing a deeper understanding of ourselves. Others you may wish to explore include the meditative forms of exercise known as t'ai chi and chi gong, as well as various Eastern martial arts, particularly aikido. The latter trains practitioners to maintain balance and serenity while facing an aggressor, using an adversary's imbalance and agitation to dissipate, redirect, or transform aggression. Many of these practices are based on the idea that there is a universal "law of being"—also called "the Tao," or "the way"—that emphasizes deep awareness of one's natural inner and outer resources as a wise and healthy way of proceeding in daily life. Based on the teachings of the venerable Chinese philosopher Lao-Tzu, the Tao's emphasis on "being" and the necessity of balance is a stark contrast to the emphasis on "doing" and self-gratifying behavior that is a hallmark of Western ideologies.

Some forms of mindfulness practice in the Sufi tradition of Islam, emphasize (and celebrate) the common messages and precepts of many of the world's religious and spiritual movements, including Christianity, Judaism, Buddhism, Hinduism, Taoism, animism, and Islam, as well as the beliefs of such indigenous groups as the Navajo, Hopi, and Pueblo people. Some Sufi groups practice a form of "body prayer" that synthesizes dance, singing, and music. Known as the Dances of Universal Peace, these gatherings are open to the public in many cities and scheduled regularly throughout the year.

Major religious traditions also incorporate some form of prayer, meditation, devotional singing, chanting, music-making, and invocation of the spirit through music or ritual. Some of these, such as the centering prayer and Quaker meetings of certain types of Christianity, are similar in form and content to the mindfulness meditation practices that have emerged from Buddhism and Taoism. Each promotes the cultivation of silence and solitude as nonmandatory prerequisites for attentive listening to the mind, body, and spirit. Through a process of balancing, these strategies can lead us to the silence and solitude of our own souls.

CHAPTER SIX

MORE SIMPLICITY, LESS STUFF; SLOWER MOVEMENT, BETTER HEALTH

As we continue to pave the world with sound,
we will continue to crave what little silence
escapes us, an emptiness made audible by its
disappearance.

—Mark Slouka, *Harper's* magazine
essay, April 1999

If silence and solitude could be bottled and sold, I am sure they would. In no time, a silence and solitude bottlers association would emerge. We would see TV commercials for silence and solitude bottled under fancy names, imported from the Swiss Alps, Hawaiian rainforests, or Alaskan glaciers. Generic bottles of the low-grade stuff would be sold in supermarkets next to no-name colas. People who had the most money would enjoy the most (and best) quiet alone-time. Sadly, billions of poor folks around the world would go without silence and solitude, except for whatever might be distributed to them through charities and religious groups.

I am thankful this scenario will never occur, although one might argue that the very absence of silence and solitude in much of the world is a direct result of the fact that no monetary profit is made when people go off quietly by themselves and do nothing. On this planet, at this time, making such a choice can be a revolutionary act. At the least, disappearing in order to be mute and alone seems odd to most folks.

Imagine how different things would be if even a small percentage of the world's population embraced silence and solitude each day. The implications are enormous: a slower pace of life, kinder public discourse, healthier bodies, sharper minds, more productive work, less violence, better-loved children, and happier individuals of all ages. As a consequence of more contemplation and reflection, found during quiet alone-time, people might take better care of themselves—and others. They might find the time to enjoy their lives more, and to honor their highest values.

Since the collapse of Communism in the 1980s, nearly all of the world's countries, whether they profess allegiance to market capitalism or not, have embraced a single creed: consumerism. The post-World War II buying binge that exploded in the United States spread to Canada, Europe, Japan, Australia, and other affluent regions where about one-sixth of the Earth's population lives. Today conspicuous consumption is a global pastime, even in countries previously considered "Third World." From Moscow to Beijing, Lima to Ho Chi Minh City, people are trying to earn more in order to—what else?—buy as many products and services as they can. Silence and solitude are definitely not among them.

How much is enough? It's a question that most of us—no matter what our age, hometown, or income—cannot answer. As the Pew Global Stewardship Initiative concluded in a 1996 report, Americans above all "cherish the ability to consume more than people elsewhere and many perceive their ability to consume at high levels as an earned privilege." In other words, we work and spend because we believe it is our personal duty and a way of preserving our country's self-image as the richest in history.

For those of us seeking silence and solitude—neither of which get much attention in a culture devoted to unbridled consumption—hope remains. An increasing number would rather enjoy some quiet alone-time than take another sweep through the marketplace.

"Many have already begun the search for a more conscious balance," wrote Ram Dass, a spiritual leader who began his career during the 1960s as Harvard psychology professor Richard Alpert. In the introduction to Duane Elgin's book, *Voluntary Simplicity*, Ram Dass suggests that a significant and growing number of Americans have found "a simplicity of living that allows the integration of inner and outer, material and spiritual, masculine and feminine, personal and social, and all of the other polarities that now [otherwise] divide our lives."

These words were written before Ram Dass suffered a stroke in 1997 that made it difficult for him to talk. In a 2000 interview with Sara Davidson for the *New York Times,* Ram Dass said his stroke gave him a fresh appreciation of silence. "I can have clear thoughts but no words for them," he explained, in the soft, halting voice that has replaced the joke-strewn glibness that once led admirers to dub him "the stand-up guru." Now when he speaks, "every once in a while—[there is] silence."

During lectures, Ram Dass invites members of his audience to join him in a place where words don't arise instantaneously. "When he fell quiet," Davidson noted, after attending such an event, "a peacefulness seemed to descend on the room as people relaxed with him." Such quiet can not only calm the mind, but change one's relationship to silence. In a similar fashion, many people have shown a remarkable ability to change their relationship with materialism. When the urge to consume decreases, and space opens in a person's life as a result, it is easier for that individual to experience some silence and solitude each day.

I went through my own metamorphosis when I gave up my big city job to enjoy a relaxed lifestyle in a much smaller community. I was amazed at how much discretionary time became available, from the two hours expended each day commuting to the time saved not buying (and dry-cleaning) a fancy corporate wardrobe. The money and effort spent maintaining my "old life," including frequent business trips, had drained me in ways I never understood until I explored my newfound quiet alone-time. Increasingly, this is a route to self-fulfillment that many others are taking.

In 1999, the Merck Family Fund disclosed that 28 percent of Americans it surveyed had "downshifted," changing their lives in ways that brought them less income but more balance and lower levels of anxiety. When asked what would make them more satisfied with their lives, most respondents wanted "less stress" and "more time with family and friends." A majority conceded that while they had more money and possessions than their parents had at their age, they did not consider themselves happier. Working women lamented that they did not have "enough time to do it all."

Experts in simplifying busy lives—and in this era there really are professional "life-simplifiers"—have plenty of suggestions for the overloaded and silence-deprived among us. Victoria Moran, author of *Shelter for the Spirit,* suggests "saying 'no' to gadgets you won't use, clothes you don't wear, and activities that aren't genuinely meaningful to you." Instead of doing marginally necessary chores like waxing the kitchen floor, Moran advises us to put people and pets first, then prioritize other obligations. Life's lowest priorities, she points out, tend to drift into insignificance and are seldom missed when ignored.

As you would expect, the voluntary simplicity movement has its detractors. Some say they enjoy their creature comforts so much that they are happy to do whatever it takes to buy them. A lucky few have enough money to remain high-level consumers without working at all. Others equate simplicity with poverty. If a person grew up in an atmosphere of scarcity, or was made to feel self-denial was morally superior to indulgence, he or she may want to feel unrestricted as an adult consumer.

But doing with *less* does not necessarily mean doing *without*. Millions of Americans feel fulfilled, content, and enriched by lifestyles that are not lavish, whether by design or circumstance. They live happily within their modest economic means. Some of those who embrace voluntary simplicity may truly have no interest in many of the goods and services available to them. Others make extensive use of what they already have, whether it is a small CD collection or a tiny backyard. Still others make sure they derive as much pleasure as possible from the indulgences they allow themselves. For anyone who lives simply, silence and solitude are cost-free options for enhancing life—just as they are for those with lots of money and worldly goods.

For someone who places a high value on financial wealth and material possessions, voluntary simplicity might look like a life constricted by painful and unnecessary limits. "Why should I deprive myself?" such a person may ask. "Why should I make do with less?" But those who make a choice of living simply—perhaps with regular quiet alone-time—are not necessarily suffering deprivation. Rather, they make choices that reflect a personal set of priorities, which may emphasize the value of *direct experience* over acquiring *physical things*. One must be careful about making moral judgments about such values, since they tend to shift in the course of a lifetime, based on changes in our attitudes.

Stevie Abbott-Richards, for example, knew when lifestyle changes were needed to bring her behavior more in sync with her beliefs. At fifty, the Australian woman was determined to make the second half of her life more inwardly rewarding than the first. "I was very ready to start over and give myself an easier run," she wrote in an essay published by the Lama Foundation, a New Mexico retreat center where she went to "get off the carousel" for a while. This in itself was a big step for someone who had spent many years as a single-parent with a full-time job.

Before her quiet alone-time at Lama, "I never had the time to consider anything in depth," noted Abbott-Richards, a former high school teacher and counselor. "Life was running me instead of the other way around."

Abbott-Richards changed hats so often that she felt like a circus juggler. At the end of each busy week, she wrote, with all the hats back on their respective pegs, "thoughts of one's life path, one's soul journey, one's self-actualization, become very hazy and 'following one's bliss' usually means taking a hot bath and then sipping a cup of tea in bed."

Like many of us, Abbott-Richards led such a revved-up, commitment-saturated life that any spare time was used for escape. Watching TV sitcoms was one way she decompressed. It took emptying her nest, selling her house, quitting her job, and flying halfway around the world for Abott-Richards to finally sit down and let the soothing solitude of the Rocky Mountains wash the "busy-ness" out of her mind, body, psyche, and spirit. Once she stopped and felt at peace with herself, the decisions necessary to live a simpler life became obvious.

What makes a simple life "simple?" We're tempted to judge such an existence by the range, quality, and complexity of its activities and tasks. Yet, even for the rich and famous, much of what fills daily life, from driving a car to tapping a keyboard, is not terribly complex. Furthermore, the variety and scope of common tasks is painfully limited. In this sense, our lives already *are* simple.

The simplicity associated with quiet alone-time has less to do with the *kinds* of activities we pursue than with their *number* and the *hours* they occupy. When we do too much, our lives are complicated and overwhelming. Paralysis, depression, or hopelessness may stop us in our tracks. Even when we limit ourselves to routine or necessary activities, following fewer of them may help us realize that our lives can be easier, simpler, and more satisfying.

Within two weeks of retreating to the woods, my life became dramatically less complicated. With so many of my usual choices decided for me by circumstance—I could neither drive to a store, for example, nor rent a movie—I studied life's most fundamental and intimate details. Aspects of basic tasks took on new meaning as I looked at them more closely.

JANUARY 31—DAY 13

An odd, disjointed day. I swept, cleaned, laundered, and chopped wood. In midday the clouds thickened and a series of snow showers swept over the ridge. There was little accumulation, and I was treated to the typically New Mexican phenomenon of the sun shining brightly while big, shimmering flakes of snow filled the air, flying to the ground in a horizontal direction: west to east. The snowflakes reflected tiny, flashing rainbow prisms of light.

I've made an excellent potato-corn-and-mixed-vegetable soup, spiked with delectable green chile. My only regret was that I had no one to share this tasty concoction with. Still, I felt triumphant for creating such an impeccably flavored soup.

LIVING AND LOVING
THE SIMPLE LIFE

Many articles and books advocate a simpler, slower lifestyle. A common theme is to cut down on clutter—and not just the physical kind—to spend more time and energy on your highest priorities, including quiet alone-time. Here are some specific suggestions:

- Schedule personal retreats. If your days are busy, write periods of "nondoing" into your datebook. Make it a point to experience silence and solitude, away from TV, phone, e-mail, and computer. You may want to sit in stillness, commune with nature, or stretch out on the couch.

- Say "no" to new demands. Politely, but firmly, turn down requests for commitments that hold little meaning for you. Such "social clutter" you can easily do without. If these refusals cost you "friendships," they are likely to be ones you won't miss.

- Get rid of things you don't want or use. They not only take up space, they require energy to manage and are draining to look at. Go through closets, dressers, cabinets, bookshelves, kitchens, garages, and even cars, selling or giving away the junk that weighs you down.

- For one month, try buying only what you need. This doesn't mean sacrificing pleasure or celebration, but focusing primarily on essential foods, clothing, prescriptions, and so on. The experiment may help you realize how much of what you buy is nonessential, potentially saving you time, money, and energy in the long run.

One of the biggest fears we may harbor about simplifying our lives is that we will have too *much* quiet alone-time on our hands. Boredom, loneliness, melancholy, sleepiness, stagnation, and restlessness may loom as larger threats than free-floating anxiety about our overflowing calendars. Without external distraction, we may worry that internal stimuli may be insufficient to hold our own fickle attention. The aversive feeling underlying this is that silence will mean helpless emptiness, that being alone will mean restless panic.

However, many who have ventured into the linked realms of silence, simplicity, stillness, and solitude dismiss such fears as groundless. Time, they assert, has an uncanny capacity to expand or contract to accommodate what we put in (or take out) of it. When we move slower, we see what otherwise passes by in a blur. When we really listen, we hear what arises within. Like tuning in a distant radio station in order to hear its message clearly, we finally know what our heart is saying. When we allow ourselves to be present in the activity at hand, we may transcend time altogether.

An engaged, dream-like sense of timelessness, Pico Iyer noted in a 1999 *Civilization* magazine essay, is "akin to what each of us feels when we are lost in something: in jogging along the beach, tending to a loved one, or being lost in concentration, feeling found and fuller than ever." You may feel this way when you are absorbed by a compelling activity: watching a gripping movie, reading a good book, cooking a favorite meal, making love passionately, or playing with happy children.

The complete absorption that Iyer describes involves an emptying out of ourselves, while at the same time filling the soul with the experience of whatever we are doing. We may be led to such experiences through our own conscious effort, but this luminous, liquid flow of time also occurs partly because of the way our brains work. When our minds are nonstriving, relaxed in a deep pool of silence and solitude, neurologists believe our brains often veer into a particular wave pattern known as "theta." This is familiar as the soft, gentle reverie that occurs just before we fall asleep. It is an effortless, uncensored way of being. I think of it as a slipstream mode where past and future—time itself—become less important.

The three-way linkage between quiet alone-time, the biological functioning of the brain, and stress-related health problems is well understood, though its complexities are still being unraveled. The basics of these interactions build a convincing argument for a regular embrace of silence and solitude grounded in their contributions to well-being and fitness alone. Many who claim they *feel* healthier when they have consistent quiet alone-time are, in fact, *in* better shape because of it.

The physiological explanation for this phenomenon involves such disparate elements as memory and immunity. In normal brain function, short-term stress enhances memory by producing a small but useful increase in glucose, which the brain draws upon as fuel. But long-term stress yields an over-secretion of the adrenal hormone cortisol, which can interfere with the brain's ability to use glucose. Too much cortisol can also interrupt production of crucial neurotransmitters that carry messages between brain cells. Even worse, chronic stress reduces the body's ability to turn off cortisol production after a stressor goes away, resulting in damaging effects on the brain, including a decline in its capacity to signal the immune system to fight disease microbes.

Studies show that periods of silence and solitude, as experienced during yoga or meditation, can lower cortisol levels (see Recommended Sources). This, in turn, may lower the impact that chronic stress has on the brain of a person whose lifestyle is ordinarily filled with stressors. In other words, the body's physical response to quiet alone-time causes it to both work and think better.

There is mounting clinical evidence that, for many practitioners, an embrace of silence and solitude has multiple positive impacts on mental well-being. For instance, a study by research psychiatrist Dr. Jean A. Hamilton, sponsored by the National Institutes of Mental Health and reported by the *New York Times* in 1989, found that those who felt more absorbed by activities—as during a timeless flow state associated with an embrace of silence and solitude—used less mental energy than did other people. It was easier for subjects to concentrate on a task, resulting in a more efficient, less stressful use of their brain.

The sense that time is flexible underscores what a relative concept this human-made abstraction really is. I once heard a radio interview with a U.S. astronaut who spent five months orbiting Earth in a space station. The man pointed out that, from his unusual vantage point, the sun rose and set every forty-five minutes. The human notion of time, in twenty-four-hour cycles of day and night, is meaningless in space. The astronaut confessed that he—and his body—never got used to this change. Without day and night our Earth-bound experience of time falls apart.

THE TIMELESSNESS OF OUR MORTALITY

For some of us, a timeless sensation emerges when we let go of our back-of-the-mind preoccupation with death. Author and hospice counselor Stephen Levine, in *One Year to Live,* describes a welcome but unanticipated byproduct of his deliberate decision to live one year as if it were his last.

"My sense of time changed," Levine wrote. "There seems to be *more* of the present. A newfound energy has been liberated . . . my relationships with friends have deepened . . . afflictive emotions have become considerably less cumbersome, and love is more available and sustainable. It feels as though I have made peace with my life."

This kind of reaction is commonly reported by individuals who have had a close brush with death, myself included. I have been in several traffic situations in which my demise seemed imminent. Even a close call while driving is sometimes enough to shift our perception of what's important, and lead us toward rewarding periods of contemplation and reflection in silence and solitude.

I came to measure time the same way millions of humans did before the Industrial Revolution: by the movement of the stars, planets, and moon across the heavens, as well as the changing angles of the sun. Time became circular, matching the recurring cycles of celestial bodies as they spun through the sky. After months of living this way, I now understand why tribal people describe events unfolding within a rotating wheel of time rather than the linear "continuum" of modern society. Upon returning to the "real world," I felt that much of the activity filling our days and nights distanced us unnecessarily from our enjoyment of it. It's as if our rushing around and multitasking creates a screen between reality and our sensory perception of that reality.

For many who choose a more serene and less "busy" lifestyle, a presumed advantage is being able to relate to the passage and utility of time differently. Time becomes a friend rather than an enemy. In a 1998 interview with the *Santa Fe New Mexican,* Robert Francis Johnson, an ecology psychologist who teaches workshops on voluntary simplicity advised, "Slow down and do one thing at a time. Wherever you are in life, take time to really be there."

PERCEIVED ADVANTAGES AND DISADVANTAGES OF A SIMPLER LIFE

Everyone has subjective reasons for downsizing and simplifying, but common themes emerge from the experiences of those who have chosen (or rejected) this route. Based on your own needs, desires, and preferences, what would you add to these lists?

Advantages

• *Easier access to silence and solitude.*

• *More discretionary time.*

• *Reduction in stress and stress-related health problems, such as heart disease and chronic back pain.*

• *Ability to save money, including money once spent on debt and interest payments for things no longer desired.*

• *Conservation of the Earth's limited resources.*

• *Less worry about where to put stuff.*

Disadvantages

• *Sacrifice of genuine needs and desires.*

• *Risk of feeling less happy than before.*

• *Loss of feelings of entitlement and freedom that come with unfettered consuming.*

• *Inability to give as much, materially, to spouse, friends, and family members.*

• *Conviction that life is too short to go without material pleasures.*

For many people, deliberate simplicity becomes its own reward. This is because one complication in our life often leads to more complications. If I decide to buy a new car that I cannot really afford, for example, I may have to take a job that requires a new wardrobe, longer commute, and rearranging my schedule to accommodate my children's school hours, my spouse's job demands, and my exercise routine. In order to pay for the new vehicle, I may have to give up entirely some things that make my life more enjoyable, such as going to movies, eating in nice restaurants, or spending leisurely mornings doing yoga or meditation. Before long, this single complication may have a far-reaching ripple effect. In the end, I may have to ask myself, "Why did I want that fancy SUV in the first place?"

One of the most difficult things about simplifying our lives is going against cultural imperatives. We are encouraged to identify with our possessions and to regard what we "own" as important. In industrialized countries, we measure our worth in material terms: the size of our house, the design of our clothes, the make of our car. But that's not all: we acquire and hold on to things for emotional reasons. As I write this, for example, I am storing a fancy, solid cherry-wood table and set of chairs that belonged to my parents. I do not use this furniture and probably never will, but its sentimental value discourages me from getting rid of it. Similarly, I have paintings I never hang on the wall because I treasure their associations, not their images. I assign meaning to such things that cannot be measured, or even seen.

When we simplify, we confront one of life's biggest bugaboos: attachment. Just as we get used to stimulation and amusement, dreading the thought of being quiet and alone, we can feel so connected to the memories (or future plans) associated with "things" that we refuse to relinquish them.

Even when the kids are grown up and gone, we may not want to leave the big house we raised them in. A pertinent late-1990s survey by the AARP estimated that nearly two out of three Americans over fifty would buy the same size home they currently live in, while 14 percent would buy an even *bigger* house. All that clinging carries a price tag. When we are unable to move stuff out of our lives, we have difficulty moving anything into them.

Vicki Robin and the late Joe Dominguez discussed the hidden costs of consumption-oriented lifestyles in their book, *Your Money or Your Life,* which advocates a simpler, less hectic existence. Drawing from their own experiences and those of other downsizers, the authors challenged readers to ask: "How much of your precious time and energy does it really cost to buy goods and services?" By figuring out how many hours of our employed labor it might take to, say, buy a new as opposed to a used car, a person could determine the "life cost" of such a purchase in addition to the dollar amount. The disparity can be sobering.

"Studies show that we [Americans] are no happier now than we were in 1957," Vicki Robin told an *E* magazine interviewer in 1996, citing a national survey by the Merck Family Fund. The survey concluded that the "happiness" index had fallen well below the 33 percent reported during the 1950s. This was "long before there were microwaves in every kitchen and computers in every bedroom," Robin noted. "We've hit a happiness ceiling."

In Robin's opinion, we may be happier enjoying the free time available as a result of spending less for something or foregoing it altogether. With more time at our disposal, she noted, we may find other like-minded people who do not mind trading or sharing goods and services. If you have access to something for free, Robin pointed out, you are less inclined to buy it.

Another advantage of having additional discretionary time is the ability to fix items that are broken, to comparison-shop for high-value bargains, to track down used goods, and to do things like grow your own food, make your own gifts, or borrow books from the library instead of buying them new. More unstructured hours also may lead us to enjoy more "quality time" with children, spouses, pets, plants, and friends, which, in turn, may reduce our spending on restaurant meals, travel, and other entertainments. We may get to know our community better, visiting galleries, museums, parks, picnic areas, and neighborhood attractions. Once we pull out of the loop of overwork and overconsumption, we become aware of an array of opportunities in life, including some we may not have explored because of economic reasons.

TEN WAYS TO SLOW THE PACE OF LIFE

Robert Francis Johnson has taught "simple living" workshops in a number of U.S. cities. He recommends, above all, taking time to think about what is really *important to you. Be mindful and vigilant, Johnson adds, of where your time and money go. What follows is an adaptation of his suggestions for slowing things down enough for silence and solitude to find a place in daily life:*

- *Stop "multitasking." For example, don't talk on the phone when you are absorbed in doing something else, whether it's folding the laundry or making dinner.*

- *Go on a media fast. Do without TV, radio, magazines, and newspapers for a week and see if your life feels different.*

- *Don't let the telephone control you. If you don't want to be interrupted, don't answer the phone or unplug it.*

- *For ten minutes to a half hour each day, sit quietly without doing anything else.*

- *Listen to music. Sit down and really listen, without multitasking.*
- *Keep a journal. Through writing, try to understand yourself better.*
- *Rediscover a childhood pleasure. Did you like blowing bubbles? Do it again.*
- *Enjoy some quality time with your pet. You will both be better off.*
- *Have a real conversation. Listen attentively to someone else, and, in turn, share your thoughts with that person.*
- *Be. Even while "doing," try to stay fully aware of feelings, senses, thoughts, and so on.*

In Europe, a social vanguard similar to the simple living trend—and also linked to silence and solitude—took hold in the late 1980s. The "Slow Food" movement, which advocates slowing down through leisurely eating, was born in Italy after the controversial 1986 opening of a McDonald's restaurant in Rome. Distressed by the prospect of a world overtaken by generic fast food, chef Carlo Petrini founded Slow Food on the proposition that life should include "an adequate portion of sensual gourmandise pleasures, to be taken with slow and prolonged enjoyment." The movement has been further defined by three guiding principles: a right to pleasure, a right to nonstandardized food (on the assumption that cuisine is a vital cultural language), and a right to slowness.

Slowness, one advocate told *Condé Naste Traveler* magazine in June 1999, is "like homeopathic medicine: If you take it in small doses every day, you will be healthier—both physically and psychically—and more attentive to the beauty of creation." Proponents of Slow Food disdain the frenzied search for profit and efficiency that has emerged since the 1980s. They decry the way productivity experts have extended their focus to food, resulting in the unvaried and unimaginative ways it is grown, prepared, presented, and eaten. Slow, sensual pleasures like dining make us happy, Slow Food advocates insist, and when we feel such pleasure we tend to have good relations with others as well as ourselves.

The Slow Food movement, with its passion for full enjoyment of life's sensual delights, brings to mind the prophetic words of Arnold Toynbee in *Change and Habit: The Challenge of Our Time:* "Civilizations in decline are consistently characterized by a tendency toward standardization and conformity." Conversely, the historian wrote, "during the growth stage of civilization the tendency is toward differentiation and diversity."

A movement similar to Slow Food applies similar sensibilities to our experience of the great American outdoors. The Quiet Use Coalition, based in Colorado's Rocky Mountains, promotes "quiet, ecologically sound means of nonmotorized recreation on our public lands and waters." Members of the nonprofit group help protect the existing naturally quiet "soundscape" on public lands and waters while establishing new silent areas on others. In a quixotic spirit reminiscent of Slow Foodists, Quiet Users are pushing against a tide that seeks to turn many U.S. parks into havens for those whose inherently loud recreational activities, from water-skiing to snowmobiling, disturb the peace for everyone within miles.

EXPLORING THE SENSUAL PLEASURES OF SILENCE AND SOLITUDE

Among the first casualties of a too-busy life are the simple, sensory enjoyments that often do not survive in the fast lane. When you find time to be quiet and alone, even for a half hour or less, such fragile pleasures may be rediscovered. They are part of what can make life feel more complete and satisfying. Suggestions for experiencing these small ecstasies include:

- *Listen to the small sounds of your household that trigger positive feelings in you: someone singing, children playing, your spouse or partner laughing, a pet making its familiar quirky noises, or someone engaged in a favorite hobby or pastime.*

- *Close your eyes and take a memory trip in your mind to a time and place that brought special enjoyment to you. Ask yourself, "What did it look, smell, feel, and sound like?" "What tastes, textures, and emotions are associated with this experience?" "Can I re-create this wondrous time and hold it inside of me?"*

- *Do some things differently that you usually do in a distracted or off-hand manner. Specifically, try doing them alone and without speaking. This might include taking a walk, preparing and eating a meal, bathing, exercising, and listening to music you like. Notice whether the sensitivity of your senses is heightened or your mind is more engaged and attentive.*

- *If you have someone in your life who is willing and interested, try making love in a silent, yet demonstrably affectionate way. Without*

*words, you may discover that other ways of communicating—through
eye contact, smelling, touching, and body language, for instance—may
take on new meaning.*

• *In your bubble of quiet alone-time, note the ways you appreciate yourself. Give yourself credit for who (and how) you are. Mentally note
your best qualities, including aspects that others who are around you a
lot (i.e., spouse, family members, colleagues, boss) seem to undervalue.
If you like parts of your body, acknowledge that, too, opening your eyes
to take them in.*

Ironically, the financial downturns that occasionally plague the modern global economy may be the biggest single reason that so many people are now choosing a simpler, more peaceful life. When jobs are lost or
salaries and benefits are cut, thousands of workers frequently discover
they can make do with less. More significantly, they often find their lives
leading them in new, more satisfying directions.

A 1995 *New York Times* article concluded that "getting laid off in middle age and mid-career can trigger a reappraisal of bedrock values."
Reporter Jennifer Stainhauer wrote how some who had lost their jobs
had determined "that the race for prestige and possessions is a sham."
One laid-off executive told the *Times:* "[Getting dismissed] was very
painful. But it was the best thing that ever happened to me."

In the final analysis, it does not matter how we come to a better
appreciation of a simpler life or the increased access to silence and solitude that often accompanies it. Whether we are fired, quit, or decide to
stay home for one reason or another, the potential benefits remain the
same.

"Simplicity depends more on the state of our minds—our inner
landscape—than on what surrounds us," concluded Ani Tuzman, director of The Dance of the Letters Writing Center in a March 1996 *Body,
Mind, Spirit* magazine article. "The key to simplicity is a quiet, contented
mind." For Tuzman, being aware in the present moment is what clears
her mental clutter.

"To be quiet and content is not to be complacent or resigned," she
wrote. "There is great clarity and power in the experience of inner
simplicity that in fact inspires us to change what needs changing within
us and in our lives. A quiet mind is the best home we can find, and we
can live there no matter where we find ourselves."

In the hushed haven of solitude, our potential discoveries run the gamut. It is important to reiterate that dramatic and far-reaching changes are not the invariable outcome of an examined life. We may find ourselves generally content with the way things are and demand few, if any, adjustments to the way we are already living. There is no rule that requires such a response. Your life already may be the way you like it. If it is not, be kind and gentle with yourself, and welcome whatever you find much as you would an unexpected house guest who arrives with the best intentions.

THE HIGH COST OF AFFLUENCE

The price we pay for a busy, affluent lifestyle is measured not only in dollars. The cost sometimes includes compromised health, strained relationships, and negative impacts on the natural environment. Plenty of sobering statistics illustrate this point.

- According to the Spring 2000 issue of *Psychosomatic Medicine,* a survey by State University of New York found that American men age thirty-five to fifty-seven who took annual vacations were 21 percent less likely to die young than nonvacationing men of the same age, and 32 percent less likely to die of coronary heart disease. The same study found that high cholesterol and hypertension raised the heart disease death rates for the vacationing men by only one to three percent.

- Each week, the average American parent spends six hours shopping versus forty minutes playing with his or her children. Kids learn from this example. In a 1996 survey reported in *Time for Life* by John P. Robinson and Geoffrey Godbey, 93 percent of teenage girls questioned said "shopping" was their favorite pastime.

- More than one-half of all children surveyed in the late 1990s by Texas A&M University marketing professor James McNeal said they would rather shop at a mall than go for a hike. According to McNeal's study, the average six-year-old participated in three shopping trips a week and children aged twelve and under made an average of fifteen requests for merchandise on each such visit.

CHAPTER SEVEN

STOPPING WHILE MOVING

Who is it that can make muddy water clear?
No one.
    But left to stand, it will gradually clear of
itself.

—Lao-Tzu, *Tao Te Ching*

n 1983, I saw a new avante-garde movie called *Koyaanisqatsi*. Walking out of a Los Angeles theater, I felt dazed and confused. What was this brilliant amalgam of clashing sounds and discordant images trying to tell me? The film showed speeded-up sequences of rush hour traffic creeping along overcrowded freeways, like blood cells straining through clogged arteries. It showed beleaguered masses in India and China, struggling to walk along jammed sidewalks. There were strip mines in Africa, shrimp farms in Ecuador, and oil fields in Kuwait. All this was intercut with footage of pristine natural beauty, including tropical rainforests, calving glaciers, and empty oceans. Koyaanisqatsi contained no actors or dialogue, only the juxtaposition of opposing images against a mesmerizing soundtrack.

"The title means 'life out of balance' in the language of the Hopi, an ancient Indian tribe of the American Southwest," critically acclaimed filmmaker Godfrey Reggio told me five years later, when I interviewed him for *Crossroads,* a public radio program. A former college teacher in the Catholic Christian Brothers order, Reggio wanted to alert moviegoers to the disruption of balance within traditional human cultures and natural systems by the "tremendous forces of modern technology, all in the name of progress and development." In Reggio's view, "Earth itself is a life-form, not raw material to be consumed and made into a synthetic world."

Some months after our conversation, I visited the Hopi reservation, in northeastern Arizona, and learned of their shared concern that, because of human intervention, life on planet Earth is seriously out of balance. Still later, I drew the conclusion that on an individual level, each of us must struggle to keep our equilibrium. "If we cannot," a Hopi elder had told me, "how can we expect the other living things in this world to do the same thing?"

Developing and maintaining a healthy balance may be one of life's most difficult and unrelenting challenges. Yet sages, psychologists, shamans, physicians, and spiritual leaders long have advised that our happiness and health depend on a suitable and recurring mix of love, exercise, food, pleasure, sleep, friendship, and other basic needs. A lack of same may lead to depression, or a lesser-known malady called anhedonia (from the

Greek, meaning "without enjoyment"). The latter, which manifests itself through such symptoms as impotence, lethargy, and indigestion, is defined in the *Random House Dictionary* as "a loss of interest or pleasure in all, or almost all, usual activities and pastimes." Put simply, those who suffer this condition are unenthused about life. I suspect millions of us suffer from this disorder to one degree or another, largely because we are too busy, too out of balance, to enjoy life. Too much of our time is taken up with one or two activities—earning money or meeting the needs of our children, for example—while too little is devoted to everything else, including quiet alone-time.

A lopsided approach to daily existence is the antithesis of a basic tenet of several major spiritual traditions—including Buddhism—that advocate "a middle way." Think of this as a lifestyle that is free of ongoing extremes and grounded instead in living in a moderate, reasoned, and sustainable manner. As a philosophy, the middle way is practical and prudent. When it comes to such basics as money, food, shelter, love, exercise, and sex, for instance, the idea is not to settle for so little that we are always striving, nor to have so much that we suffer the negative consequences of overindulgence. In the embrace of quiet alone-time, as an integral part of a balanced reality, we have the chance to weigh the sustainability of what we have in life.

The modern world tends to steer us toward extremes, notably at work. The obsessive behavior we see around us is fueled by a cultural dictum that happiness is found largely through productivity, materialism, and distraction, paid for by working long hours at jobs that aren't what we enjoy. The old adage "all work and no play makes a dull boy" falls on deaf ears.

The ancient Greeks and Romans are said to have honored balance to such an extent that they had specific words in their languages to describe the appropriate blend of ingredients in an ideal life. English does not, which in itself is revealing. The medicine and wisdom traditions of China and India, as well as tribal cultures throughout the world, have long praised the value of equanimity, an evenness of temperament and energy. For centuries, Asian doctors have sought a balance of "life force" in the human body as a way of treating illness and maintaining robust health. This contrasts with modern Western medicine that responds to physical *symptoms* rather than *root causes*. In Africa, where humans are believed to have originated, mythic stories describe the need for us to emulate the natural world, in which conflicting forces reach a state of equilibrium that sustains ecological systems in a health-promoting manner. On every inhabited continent, generations of indigenous people have flourished through adherence to "the middle way."

A key element in the balanced life is flexibility. When we become rigid, locked into extreme behavior (like pathological overwork), we tend to reject alternatives. The workaholic may see no way of changing his or her behavior, or may dismiss other lifestyles reflexively, anticipating being unable to satisfy his or her perceived needs. When we become addicted to work, silence and solitude lose their place and are unable to serve as a counterweight to rigid views and patterns.

"The belief that things can't change is central to the logic of addiction," one-time gang member, alcoholic, and drug abuser Luis Rodríguez told a *Sun* magazine interviewer in 2001. "It's what keeps you trapped in the web. When you're surrounded by pathology and abuse, it's easy to feel you can never break free of that web of addictions. But it's still possible. Nobody says change is easy. It takes effort."

Rodríguez broke his own cycle of addiction through his discovery in prison of literature, which taught him that there were other ways to live. He went on to become a successful writer and publisher, although the Chicago resident spends much of his time helping troubled urban teenagers lead more balanced lives.

Whether you are a factory drone chained to an assembly line, a computer user marooned in an office cube, or a gang member confined to an urban *barrio*, there are ways to make silence and solitude a part of your daily routine. Over time, an existence without them is more likely to devolve into a life out of balance.

John Murray reinforces this conviction with precise directness in his book, *The Quotable Nature Lover*. Once in a while, Murray says, an indeterminate period of unavailability is a good idea: "Each person, each sane person, maintains a refuge, or series of refuges, for this purpose. A place, or places, where they can, figuratively if not literally, suspend their membership in the human race."

Intermittent departure from routine—even a restful walk in a city park or withdrawal from a crowded room to the serenity behind a closed door—helps us from being knocked off-kilter by the unsteadying forces that assault us during a typical day.

What social commentators hint at is something that biologists and anthropologists know very well. What makes both natural and cultural organisms able to manage change and cope with sudden trauma is their resilience and adaptability. When such beings are stressed, their flexibility allows them to move, make adjustments, and restore themselves. In a very literal sense, this is how they survive.

But humans and their civilizations, like most large animals and animal-created social systems, tend to absorb change slowly. What helps big mammals survive is their strength, cleverness, stamina, and endurance. But there are limits, as the dinosaurs found out millions of years ago when, according to the prevailing theory, a large asteroid created an environmental shock to which they could not rapidly adapt. While our species has been able to assimilate change relatively well until now, our institutions are pushing the envelope. The pace of life in which we evolved, over hundreds of thousands of years, has increased exponentially since the early 1900s, and especially since 1980. While the rest of the natural world is trying to move at the same rate it always has, human beings are trying to match the speeds of the machines they have created.

"The planet is the slowest clock," economist and social critic Paul Hawken told me during a conversation in 2001, referring to a theory advanced by Steward Brand. In contrast, "the dominant time frame [among humans today] is commercial. Businesses are quick, welcome innovation in general, and have a bias toward change. They need to grow more quickly than ever before, and they are punished, pummeled, and bankrupted if they do not." Why is this important to the average American citizen? Because, as President Calvin Coolidge reminded us in the 1920s, "the business of America is business." Even if we are not, as individuals, engaged directly in business, we are affected by its impact on our culture.

Hawken, a social activist and cofounder of both the highly successful Erewhon grocery and Smith & Hawken mail-order firms, blames "the Internet, greed, global communications, and high-speed transportation" for making businesses—and people—move faster than ever. In this so-called Information Age, he notes, getting work done quickly seems to take precedence over living a balanced, happy life.

The disequilibrium of our society is bound to have an impact on us, even if we cultivate mindfulness in daily living and manage a regular embrace of silence and solitude. This is because the things that other people do—even if we do not emulate them—influence us. Exactly how and to what degree is anybody's guess, and the impact varies from one person to another. Science is only beginning to explore this realm, but early research is illuminating.

The observations of physician Stephen Rechtschaffen provide a good example. Rechtschaffen is the author of *Timeshifting,* a book that examines the relationship between natural systems and time-related cycles. Rechtschaffen describes a documented but little-understood phenomenon he calls "entrainment," the tendency of nonsynchronized rhythms to fall in step with each other. An example you may have read about—or personally experienced—is the way menstrual cycles of women who live or work in close proximity to one another often fall into a closely aligned pattern. In some offices or households, it takes only a few months for women to discover that their periods have shifted to the same cycle. Similarly, you may have noticed the way wake-up times, which often follow rhythms dictated by sunrise, are thrown off-balance by long-distance travel or the beginning and end of daylight savings time. Music also exerts a profound influence: slow, soft melodies tend to help us relax while fast, brassy beats speed us up. This phenomenon is not limited to humans, either. Even out-of-sync ticking clocks sometimes adjust to each other without intervention.

Why is this important? Because, Rechtschaffen says, "the fast-paced rhythm of modern life conditions us to skim the surface of experience [and] then quickly move on to something new." He believes the frantic pace that is typical of current lifestyles trickles into all aspects of our lives and even affects those who try to live at a slower rhythm. The lifestyles of the majority, through the influence of "entrainment," may make it harder on those who embrace silence and solitude.

Subliminal energies and cycles also may have some bearing on the "collective unconscious" that Swiss psychologist Carl Jung believed was the repository of a kind of intuitive intelligence shared among all humans. Such phenomena may help explain why so much tribal music around the world is tuned to the rhythms of the heartbeat or the respiration of lungs, as pounded out on drums, strummed on guitars, and chanted in tones that energize both body and soul.

But the beat of modern industrialized society is one that sweeps all of us along, to some degree, regardless of personal preference and individual temperament. It is mechanical and digital, tuned to the demands of speed-of-light technologies and binary codes rather than flesh-and-blood bodies and DNA helixes. A mechanized tempo is far from natural for human beings, with the long-term consequences so far unknown.

FINDING YOUR BALANCE

The balance between alone-time and social interaction will be different from one person to another, since our intrinsic needs are never the same. Yet determining a healthy equilibrium does not have to be done on our own, even though silence and solitude can help inform that determination. We can learn about this part of ourselves in conversations with others, particularly those closest to us, and through participation in structured events, retreats, workshops, or classes that are focused on self-awareness and personal transformation, such as groups that meet regularly to both meditate and discuss that practice. Check the resources section in the back of this book for specific suggestions.

Mounting evidence, however, suggests that we ignore nature's rhythms at our peril.

In the September 1996 issue of *Smithsonian*, Joyce and Richard Wolkomir reported on a series of unusual experiments by Virginia historian Roger Ekirch and National Institutes of Mental Health psychiatrist Thomas A. Wehr in which they discovered that research subjects, when deprived of artificial light, revert to a sleep-wake pattern that was common before the Industrial Age. The subjects sleep for three or four hours at a stretch, then lie awake in bed or get up for one to three hours before returning to sleep for another three or four hours. Ekirch believes people not exposed to artificial light sleep differently because they secrete more prolactin, a pituitary hormone that promotes a blissful state of quiet restfulness. This is the same substance that allows chickens to sit contentedly atop their eggs for hours on end and accounts for the mellow mood in which many of us awaken after a full night's sleep.

The *Smithsonian* article also mentioned that other researchers based at Harvard Medical School isolated a brain chemical called adenosine as an important player in the mechanisms that make humans (and other mammals) alternately sleepy and alert, triggering their wake-sleep cycle. Caffeine—to which many of us are addicted—mitigates the influence of adenosine in the brain, chasing away our desire to sleep. Scientists believe that other activities in modern life may also block this chemical, which accumulates in our cells naturally during the course of the day. Could it be that we feel "wired" and tense because our lifestyles affect our brain chemistry in ways that disrupt natural cycles? No one yet knows for sure.

We do know, however, that because we live within a social matrix stimulated by a lot of technology—not to mention coffee and artificial light—we are influenced by the speedy, syncopated patterns surrounding us. We are like passengers on a train that others are controlling. Not only is it hard to get off the train, it is difficult to ignore what the majority of other passengers are doing. We may feel we are the only person on board who craves a slower, quieter, and less crowded ride. Everyone else may be perfectly content with the train's fast speed, or want it to travel even faster. Our fellow riders have synchronized themselves to technological rhythms. The engineer? We have no communication with this unseen pilot, who for all we know may be a robot.

Many of us are frustrated by the hurried, work-oriented focus of our society. We feel helpless and powerless. The train is not stopping, and it's going too fast for us to jump off. It feels like no one else sees the dangers that lie ahead. Such is life in the twenty-first century.

Entering the third month of my time alone in the wilderness, the rhythms of my life changed dramatically from those I was familiar with in the "real world." My days fell into a balanced pattern of physical labor and creative activity (such as writing or making art), along with contemplative practices like yoga, meditation, and chanting. Yet even after nine weeks of isolation, it was still difficult to find and maintain a balance that felt "just right." I had begun to conclude that striving for a balanced life is really an ongoing, lifelong challenge.

MARCH 25—DAY 66

I've been writing much of today, feeling anxious about the shrinking number of days I have left here. I've felt in conflict, during much of this retreat, between my desire to produce a certain amount of work on the one hand and my desire simply to be in the present on the other: attending to my spiritual practice, nature walks, disconnecting from the chattering mind, and trying to open my heart to everything that gets blocked or constricted by my intellect and inner dialogue. I've finally found a good balance, but it's been a challenge that I confront anew each day.

The imbalance and short-sightedness of modern life exacts its toll in many ways. Today's children, for example, suffer from an epidemic of physical, behavioral, and psychological problems that may be related to the ever-quickening pace and growing din of their lives and, by extension, a lack of silence and solitude. The list of symptoms includes attention deficit disorder, hyperactivity, anxiety, lack of empathy, uncontrolled anger, fragmented thinking, violent behavior, stress, erratic sleep patterns, and an inability to maintain stamina or concentration. As members of a generation raised on MTV, video games, pop music, and media sound bites, our young people get bored quickly and easily. No wonder so many of them feel apathetic toward school.

Among the harried and hurried of all ages, social critic Barbara Ehrenreich pointed out in a 1999 *New York Times* commentary, "the chance to reflect, to analyze, and, ultimately, to come up with moral judgments" is often lost. Deep concentrated thought isn't as fast as an electron or a nerve impulse. Concentration and contemplation take time—for the patterns of neural firing to shift, connect, and interact to form whole new patterns in our minds.

Faster is exhilarating, Ehrenreich concluded, "but *slower* might have got us a whole lot further along." In the long run, our ever-increasing connectedness may be making us collectively dumber, not smarter.

It does not have to be this way. In our quest for silence and solitude we can take at least two important actions. First, we can change—or at least reflect upon—our relationship with work and other obligations instead of unconsciously allowing job-related tempos to shape our own internal rhythms. Second, we can adapt to—or actively seek to alter—the conditions of our specific work environment so that it better meets our needs and desires. We may be surprised to learn that others have similar feelings and would welcome such changes as much as we would.

Going to work does not preclude participation in the realms of silence, solitude, stillness, and simplicity. "I've seen people be silent and alone, but unbelievably busy," anthropologist Joan Halifax once told me. "It's not about isolating yourself from others, from your community, or from the world, but it's knowing how to be sufficient within each of those arenas." Quiet alone-time is also not about pursuit of isolation to the degree it becomes unhealthy and dysfunctional, an important topic worthy of its own book.

ACCOMMODATING SILENCE AND SOLITUDE BY CHANGING YOUR RELATIONSHIP TO WORK

Sometimes we have no choice about being in a noisy, crowded environment. The kind of work we do may demand it. Yet even jobs like these usually can be modified so that employees can find occasional quiet alone-time. Here are a few suggestions:

- *Avoid bringing work home, either on weeknights or weekends. If you can't get your tasks done during normal work hours, take a close look at why this is so and try to address the causes effectively. If you rely on overtime as a source of income or diversion from other arenas of life, consider the implications of such reliance. Ask yourself if the sacrifices you make are really worth what you are getting back.*

- *If you have flexibility in your schedule, figure out how many of your work hours are devoted to earning money for essentials: food, clothing, shelter, and health care. Are many of your work hours going to support nonessential lifestyle expenses? If so, ask yourself if you would rather trade some of those work hours for more free time.*

- *Pay attention to how excessive noise and social interaction affect you at work. At the same time, reflect on how quiet alone-time influences you. If the latter's impact is positive, consider finding ways to increase the amount of silence and solitude available. This may involve something as simple as taking a walk around the block during a scheduled break, or finding an empty room where you can close your eyes and decompress.*

- *If your workplace is chronically noisy, try wearing earplugs or experiment with ways to shut out sound, using buffering screens, doors, window treatments, or masking devices.*

- *If the interruptions of coworkers drain and distract you, find a way to tell them, politely yet firmly, that there are times when you wish to be left alone. Develop a system (i.e., a scheduled portion of the day, a sign on your closed door) that will let them know that you are "unavailable."*

Work is not really the problem here. The key issue is how we respond and relate to our jobs (including that of parent or home-maker) and the functions they serve. In our society, most able-bodied and mentally healthy adults are expected to be employed outside the home. Our attachment to our work and our expectations from it are critical in determining how—or whether—we will choose to let quiet alone-time play a role in our busy lives. If we cannot, or do not, want to stop working long enough to decompress, it's time to examine the fundamental relationship between self and work. Perhaps it is the role we play on the job that feeds us. Maybe we are so attached to the social milieu at work that it has become a surrogate family. Even if our intentions are honorable, we may have lost sight of the other responsibilities we have in life: to family, to community, to friends, and, most important, to ourselves.

"You may have become stuck in your work role and may be unable to operate in your many other life roles comfortably," Jon Kabat-Zinn speculates in *Full Catastrophe Living*. "You may even have forgotten what is important to you. You may even have forgotten who you are." In the United States, adults are identified closely with their jobs, both in the eyes of others and in evaluations of their own self-worth. Each of us has had the experience of being asked, "What do *you* do?" immediately after being introduced to a stranger. In Western culture, one's identity (especially for men) is closely tied to one's career.

If we love what we do for a living, if it nurtures and restores rather than exhausts and depletes us, what is wrong with putting in long hours? When does willing dedication to a favorite activity (that we also happen to get paid for) cross the line into workaholism?

Our answers to these questions will depend upon whether we have a healthy equilibrium in our lives. Devoting enormous amounts of time to work, no matter how much pleasure it gives, becomes unhealthy when it downgrades, disconnects, or excludes other activities that are considered essential to a balanced life: getting regular exercise, following a nutritious diet, maintaining intimacy with other human beings, and making time to face aspects of our lives that need attending. For example, when we cannot tune in to the feelings of others, or our own, we are stuck in an unfulfilling place that may lead to serious physical and psychological health problems.

One place to tune in to our inner self is at work. There is no rule

WORKING MEDITATION

Some among us "may wish to live in a way that creates the least suffering, both for themselves and others," the revered Thai forest monk Ajahn Jumnien once noted in an interview conducted by American Buddhist teacher Jack Kornfield and retold by Kornfield at a Buddhist retreat. In order to accomplish this, Jumnien continued, such a person must "choose to live simply and cool the heart in concentration and stillness." But what comes next? Very few individuals have the commitment or desire to remain in silence and solitude indefinitely. Most of us eventually need to get back to work.

"Karma yoga" in Hinduism describes a kind of selfless employment; Buddhists call it "right livelihood." Both religions hold that one should engage in activities that benefit others, as well as one's self, and, above all, consciously do no harm. In contemporary vernacular, this is known as "walking your talk." By bringing work into alignment with underlying personal and spiritual values, life is more likely to feel "in balance." Work can become a focus of mindful attention, like following one's breath in meditation. No matter what your job, whether paid or not, it is useful to consider, perhaps during quiet alone-time, whether the work resonates with your most fundamental beliefs. If it does not, changes may be in order.

that says the American workplace must exclude the experience of silence and solitude. An increasing number of employers, in fact, have responded to requests from their employees that such access be provided. In a few cases, the owners and managers themselves are initiating the change.

In my home state of New Mexico, for example, the Western Environmental Law Center, based in Taos, has adopted a set of policies that might serve as a model for enlightened businesses that wish to preserve the sanity (and productivity) of their employees. According to attorney Grove Burnett, the center's director, the policy was prompted by the realization that personal relationships between many employees and their loved ones were suffering due to the long hours the employees devoted to their jobs.

In an interview for my January, 2000, article in the *Albuquerque Journal,* Burnett told me, "A lot of us just were not very happy. . . .There was this huge disparity between the way we aspired to live our lives—and in some cases were preaching to others that they should live theirs—and the way we actually were living them."

The Western Environmental Law Center now grants its employees paid breaks during the work day for an embrace of silence and solitude, or a contemplative practice of their choice. Once a week, staffers get together for an hour to talk about the challenges and successes of their personal lives. Discussions of work are off-limits. Once each month, all employees spend a paid work day working together on a community service project, such as making birdhouses for a nursing home or helping repair an old church. Once each year, staff members are allowed to take time off for personal retreats or sabbaticals that allow them to "recharge their batteries." Except for emergencies, employees are not allowed to work beyond five in the afternoon and must not exceed forty hours of work in any given week.

"The biggest surprise to me is not that we are happier," said Burnett, "but that we are more productive. Our employees, including me, now get more done in a forty-hour week than they used to get done in sixty or seventy hours." The attorney speculates that he and his coworkers operate with much greater efficiency when their lives are more balanced and are now less likely to take on more than they expect themselves to accomplish.

Europe and Latin America have a more relaxed and balanced approach to work than what most Americans endure. In France, for example, businesses cut work weeks to thirty-five hours after the socialist federal government decided that the eight-hour day was antiquated. According to Tim Holt citing a 2000 National Public Radio report described in the *San Francisco Chronicle,* France is the same country where one survey found many people didn't want a computer in their homes because they were considered "too corrosive to personal relations."

Not only do European workers put in fewer hours than their U.S. counterparts, they typically get two to three times as many days of paid vacation and holidays as well as other lucrative benefits, including fully subsidized health insurance and maternity/paternity leave. You won't find most Europeans working at night or on weekends, either. Many workers still roll into their offices at a civilized 9:30 A.M. and a fair number take an hour or two off for lunch (and perhaps a bit of silence, solitude, and sleep) before ending the workday around 6:30 P.M.

"In the end, you've got people who are content and happy in life, and who do their jobs properly when they're at work," summed up Roxanne Suratgar, an Italian market analyst, in a 1999 Associated Press interview.

Despite news reports and research confirming America's obsession with work, a growing number of employees are opting out of the rat race, at least temporarily. In virtually all industrialized countries, including the United States, thousands of people from all walks of life are engaged at any given time in sabbaticals or retreats that focus on spiritual or personal renewal. Many choose destinations that offer serenity, natural beauty, and isolation. Retreat centers tucked in rural areas and even big or medium-sized cities welcome those eager to experience contemplative practice or deep relaxation. For individuals and families who can't get away for this explicit purpose, vacations and three-day weekends no doubt provide some of the same rewards.

"When we feel in need of a holiday, we often refer to needing 'a change,'" wrote psychiatrist Anthony Storr in *Solitude: A Return to the Self.* "Holidays and the capacity to change march hand in hand. The word 'retreat' carries similar overtones of meaning." Storr recalls that "The Retreat" was the name given to one of the first British mental hospitals, founded in 1792 and designated a safe "asylum" from the harassments of the world.

Whether we actually *find* inner peace and stress reduction on our vacations, retreats, and weekend getaways is another matter entirely. Certainly, many people successfully relax and rejuvenate, returning to work rested and refreshed. But others are locked into a style of presumed relaxation that makes this outcome unlikely, if not impossible. Too often their holidays are too much like the rest of their lives: overbooked and overstressed. Though the standard weekend and two-to-three-week annual vacation is an accepted—almost sacred—ritual in contemporary American life, it is not conducive to reflection or contemplation. In fact, the exact opposite is the rule: our holidays are often action-packed adventures full of movement, stimulation, amusement, and interaction.

This is probably not what God had in mind when he (or she) prescribed twenty-four hours of nonwork on the seventh day of the week. In the modern era, only a small percentage of the religiously devout actually *rest* on their Sabbath days. Nor is the modern American vacation what the originators of the sabbatical had in mind when the concept of a long break from a normal career path was instituted. The word *sabbatical* derives from an Old Testament word for "Sabbath year," a time-honored agricultural practice of letting land lie fallow every seventh year. The idea is that people, like cultivated lands, are more productive when given a substantial rest every so often. Today we tend to forget—or ignore—this ancient wisdom and its underlying theme of balance.

It may seem that only professors and teachers are entitled to sabbaticals. I once met a Brooklyn schoolteacher who spent every available minute of her summer break on a sunny Greek island, where she spent a large part of each day "lying fallow" on the beach. But sanctioned long-term getaways are becoming common in all kinds of professions. According to a 2000 survey by the International Foundation of Employee Benefits, about 20 percent of U.S. companies offered unpaid sabbaticals. Major corporations offering extended leave (of three to twelve months) included IBM, Tandem Computer, and Federal Express. The models for these companies are sometimes taken from firms operating in Australia, where the concept of "long leaves" is guaranteed by the country's employee-friendly labor laws.

"A sabbatical offers multiple benefits for all sides," Vanderbilt University business professor Terrence Deal told *Escape* magazine publisher Joe Robinson in a published interview. "The individual benefits: from the opportunity to walk off the beaten path, to reflect, to encounter different cultural situations that reveal the craziness of many of the things we do. The companies benefit, because people return renewed."

Sometimes the transformations wrought by sabbaticals are profound. "I came back a totally different person," former eighty-hour-a-week mutual fund manager John Slocum told Robinson, after taking some time out from a life where Slocum confessed that all he "ever wanted to do was banking and investments. . . . I was able to think about where my life really was and focus on what made me happy and how I wanted to live." What does Slocum do now? He started an organization that helps burned-out workaholics take sabbaticals.

Recognition that time off is good for the bottom line—and people—has spread to other institutions besides businesses. Many government entities, nonprofit organizations, churches, health-care providers, and schools—even refugee camps and prisons—incorporate some form of meditative silence and sanctioned solitude in the array of services made available to those these institutions serve.

CHAPTER EIGHT

INTIMACY AND INDEPENDENCE

> The magic secret is to do just one thing at a time. We do what we're doing when we do it.
>
> —Bernie Glassman,
> *Instructions to the Cook*

Edward Abbey, the Pennsylvania-raised curmudgeon who wrote so eloquently about the harsh beauty of the American Southwest, once described a raft trip he took, alone, down a quiet stretch of the Colorado River in a remote corner of Utah. Abbey, an occasional ranger at nearby Arches National Park, conceded that he had grown churlish in anticipation of an upcoming presidential election, the expected outcome of which put him in a foul humor.

"Since I lacked the power to make a somewhat disagreeable world of public events disappear, I chose to disappear from that world myself," Abbey explained in his essay, "River Solitaire: A Daybook" published in *Down the River*. "I preferred this kind of solitude not out of selfishness, but out of generosity; in my sullen mood I was doing my fellow humans (such as they are) a favor by going away."

Each of us confronts times—bad days, or even bad weeks—when the company of our "fellow humans," even those who love us dearly, is unwelcome. We recognize that our temporary exile should not be perceived as a personal rejection of those we leave behind, inasmuch as the need to withdraw is often sparked from within and not by the actions (or presence) of others. For whatever reason, we wish to be alone. Sometimes we need solitude to discover *why* we need it, and what the urge to withdraw points toward. Many times we balance solitude with connection because we are more connected with others after taking time away from them.

For men especially, according to John Gray and others who specialize in the field of gender-differentiated psychology, there is sometimes an overwhelming desire to retreat into "the cave." By withdrawing into silence and solitude, males in modern Western society often feel better equipped to sort out and examine their thoughts and emotions. A reduction in human contact and external stimulation allows them to pay closer (and better) attention to what is at hand.

Sociolinguist Deborah Tannen points out in her groundbreaking book about the communication styles of men and women, *That's Not What I Mean!*, that "one of the most common stereotypes of American men is the 'strong silent type.'" While a posture of silence may comfort many males, Tannen notes, it tends to unnerve women, who prefer heart-to-heart talks when the going gets tough. "Women often have a relatively greater need for involvement," Tannen concludes, "and men a relatively greater need for independence."

Research suggests that solitude—physical separateness from other people—carries different implications for women than is does for men. Without anyone around to use as a reference point, a woman may feel she does not know where she stands, or even who she is. Women have traditionally been defined by their relationships to others, and social commentator Barbara Holland notes that "even today a solitary woman may feel like a tree falling in the empty forest." Deprived of interaction, her sense of identity may disappear. In silence and solitude, Holland suggests in her book, *One's Company: Reflections on Living Alone,* women "can lose the very sense of their selves." Yet women, like men, sometimes also conclude that the best way to get closer to a spouse is by retreating for a while.

What we often seek through our temporary abandonment of others is a deeper connection with our truest self. We can then reflect this *authentic* self back to others. In understanding ourselves more deeply and truthfully, the shared current of life is made more electric again.

Thomas Merton understood this concept when he wrote in *Disputed Questions* that "without solitude of some sort there is and can be no maturity. Unless [a person] becomes empty and alone, he cannot give himself in love because he does not possess the deep self which is the only gift worthy of love." Merton's view recalls the maxim that we cannot truly accept others unless we learn to accept ourselves. In loving ourselves without reservation, we are better able to love others in the same unconditional spirit. In his personal journal, this cloistered monk observed that "solitude rips off all the masks and all the disguises. It tolerates no lies."

If we want to improve our intimate relationships, we are wise to look inward first, examining our hearts, minds, bodies and spirits. On the most basic level, this is who we are. How could it not be? The self *is* our home. Having explored that realm, we can move outward, integrating others into our reality.

Each of us sometimes stands in the way of ourselves, aware of things about our attitudes or behaviors we wish were different yet feel unable to change. I can cite plenty of my own. There is my habit, for instance, of distracting myself with low-priority busywork. By being drawn to what feels comforting, I can postpone more difficult tasks.

Psychologists call this strategy of avoidance "adaptive behavior," although I believe it also may reflect our all-too-human desire to embrace that which nurtures and soothes us, while skirting obstacles in our path. During my time alone in the woods, I grappled with this two-sided pattern of avoidance and desire.

Since I was deprived of most modern conveniences at the wilderness ranch, I was forced to adapt to circumstances. This often meant either doing without or making do with "old-fashioned" technology. For example, the absence of electricity meant I had no washer, dryer, microwave oven, blender, toaster, or any other appliance except a gas-powered refrigerator, stove, and water heater. There were no electric lights, no power saws, and no flush toilets. My only snowmobile was broken and my only heat came from wood I chopped myself. Because many chores took more time and effort than I was used to, I sometimes put them off for as long as possible.

APRIL 1—DAY 72

March was the most difficult month of my adventure. I struggled with restlessness and a desire to return to my "normal" life. It depressed me that on March fifth I was only halfway through my experience of isolation. The weather was also an issue: more snow in March than in January and February combined, by far. I was tired of the cold and the white frozen expanse. I wanted to hike on bare ground, not hobble around on snowshoes, break trail with skis, or sink up to my knees in slush.

Somehow I got through that rough patch, focusing on the present, letting go of my preoccupations with the past and future, and deepening my meditative practices. I stopped "leaning" toward what happens next. With eighteen days left, I can feel the sand running more quickly into the bottom of the glass. I find myself estimating how much I can still accomplish, and how much will certainly remain undone.

The arrival of spring lifts my spirits. I love the longer days and shorter nights. The hours from 6 to 10 P.M. are still my biggest challenge, especially with the loss of my propane reading light a week or so ago. (It exploded for unknown reasons.) Now I don't have enough light to read after sunset. Writing is problematic at night and I rarely indulge. Today I did all of my laundry by hand on the washboard again, the task made easier knowing that I will only do it once or twice more.

APRIL 2—DAY 73

Another winter storm, bringing high winds and light snow from about

5 A.M. to 6 P.M. I went snowshoeing for a while, but the wind made it very cold and difficult to see.

I spent much of the day listening to music, dancing, drawing, meditating, and practicing yoga. It felt like I had achieved a breakthrough of sorts. Although I have more reading and writing to do, it occurred to me to suspend all that activity and work in body-and-spirit realms for the rest of my time here.

ONE MAN'S VIEW OF THE CHANGING RELATIONSHIP TO SELF

Wes Nisker—author, teacher, and fellow radio journalist—writes that in quiet silence we may begin to pay less attention to, or even ignore, our individual personalities. We might even move beyond them, taking the personality—the most narcissistic feature of our ego—down from its usual pedestal at the center of our being.

"And what a relief that can be," Nisker wrote in one of his *Inquiring Mind* newspaper columns. "One suggestion is to regard your personality as a pet. It follows you around anyway, so give it a name and make friends with it. Keep it on a leash when you need to, and let it run free when you think that this sort of freedom is appropriate. Train it as well as you can, and then accept its idiosyncrasies, but always remember that your pet is not *you*. Your pet has its own life and just happens to be in an intimate relationship with you, whomever you may be, hiding there behind your personality."

In one important sense, we engage in a temporary retreat from engagement with the world every night. The familiar act of going to sleep is a literal embrace of silence and solitude. Here, humans process and sort things out. In unconscious slumber—as the body recharges and the mind glides in and out of dreams—experts say we respond to unresolved anxieties, try to solve the previous day's problems, solidify memories, absorb newly acquired information, and explore our creativity. Perhaps this explains why people urge us to "sleep on it" when a difficult decision or complicated choice presents itself. It may be that we need, literally, some contact with the fertile and restorative recesses of our inner world in order for our brains to function at their best. In what may be the ultimate quiet alone-time, free from the distractions and noise of the awakened world, we turn inward to confront, integrate, and enjoy parts of ourselves that we simply do not get to experience so fully as when we are asleep.

Some researchers believe many stress-related disorders and accidents can be traced to a lack of downtime aggravated by a lack of sufficient sleep. The National Sleep Foundation estimates sleep-deprived workers cost U.S. industry $18 billion in missed workdays and lowered productivity during 2000. But today's reality is that few among us get enough rest.

"People erroneously believe they have to burn the midnight oil to succeed," Dr. Don Weaver, director of a Dallas insomnia treatment program, told a Knight Ridder reporter in 2001. "Their motto is, 'The best never rest.' The truth is, the best rest."

In 1900, according to historians, the average American adult slept eight and one-half hours each night. Today, the average is just below seven hours, with one-third of adults claiming they typically sleep less than six and one-half hours per night.

Perhaps periods of *awakened* silence and solitude, like unencumbered sleep, are also helpful—possibly even necessary—in order for us to handle fresh information, adapt to change, address confusion, consider the significance of events, and heal wounds of the heart, soul, and psyche, as well as the body. British psychiatrist Anthony Storr, writing in *Solitude: A Return to the Self,* posits that "prayer and meditation facilitate integration by allowing time for previously unrelated thoughts and feelings to interact. Being able to get in touch with one's deepest thoughts and feelings, and providing time for them to regroup themselves into new formations and combinations, are important aspects of the creative process, as well as a way of relieving tension and promoting mental health." The parallels between sleep and contemplative solitude are worth exploring, even though the potential of quiet alone-time has been largely ignored by researchers.

EXPLORING SILENCE AND SOLITUDE WHILE OTHERS ARE AWAY

If we live with others—spouse, partner, housemate, children, parents— sometimes we have the place to ourselves. The husband or wife may go off on a business trip, for example, or care for a sick relative. Children may visit grandparents or attend summer camp. Housemates may be called away for a host of reasons.

These are invaluable chances to explore silence and solitude: to see

what life is like without the constant, tethering presence of the "other."
Many of us find these intervals relaxing and welcome them as an
indulgence, a treat, or a kind of guilty pleasure. We do well to plan for
them wisely. Remember that you do not have to sit and wait for such
circumstances to present themselves—take direct action if time alone
feels like an immediate priority.

If you are normally on a rigid schedule, use your interval of home-
bound silence and solitude to come and go as you please, to stay up late,
or to rise early. Try some of the following:

• Change your patterns and break your habits.

• Eat at odd times and try new foods.

• Respond to people in ways that you (or they) would not ordinarily
expect.

• Move at a different pace.

• Sleep in a room that is not your own.

• Take a bath in the middle of the day.

• Walk around the house naked.

• Step into the backyard and sit in the sun, closing your eyes to focus on
mindful listening to your environment.

• If the weather is warm enough, consider sleeping in the yard overnight.

• Walk meditatively in circles, without destination or inhibition.

Be mindful of how you feel and what you think as you interrupt
your routines. Consider the difference between who you are now, as you
explore quiet alone-time, and who you are the rest of the time. Stop to
observe your breath, noting the thoughts and emotions that constantly
arise and float through you, like fluffy clouds drifting across an enor-
mous sky. How are the qualities of your moment-by-moment awareness
different (or the same) when no one else is in your living space, when
you know you will not be interrupted or observed?

In silence and solitude we can deepen our intimacy with others,
sometimes by getting away from them for a while. Through the self-
discovery afforded by quiet alone-time, the quality of the intimacy in our
lives evolves, becoming richer, deeper, more fulfilling. New paths present
themselves, leading to closer relations with partner or spouse, children or
siblings, other family members, or colleagues at work. Our relationship

with intimacy may change as well, perhaps becoming one of the most important outcomes of our cultivation of silence and solitude. With a new outlook on intimate relationships—including our relationship with ourselves—we may find a new sense of closeness and connection with family, friends, and coworkers.

I felt this enhanced and expanded intimacy after I returned from my winter at the ranch. Although it had its drawbacks, including an emotional sensitivity almost too strong to bear at times, the openness of my heart was a gift that I cherished. One of the most difficult aspects of my transition was dealing with my former girlfriend's decision to take up with a new man during my absence. Despite the pain we both felt, Kate and I developed a stronger friendship as a result of the openness I felt and my willingness to be "present" for whatever life offered. Extended quiet alone-time had made me less attached to the outcome of my relationship with her, even though we were saddened that our romance was over. After readjusting to my new reality, I knew I would be open to meeting someone new.

The cultivation of deep intimacy is one of the most sought-after goals in human life. Many believe that a yearning for closer connection is at the heart of what really motivates us, pushing us to know—and be known—more completely. According to Barbara Holland in *One's Company,* writer Don Marquis put the matter succinctly when he declared that "all religion, all life, all art, all expression come down to this: the effort of the human soul to break through its barriers of loneliness, of intolerable aloneness, and make some contact with another seeking soul."

But what is deep intimacy? How can I become more intimate with another without losing intimacy with myself? How can I balance my need for independence with my need for closeness? These are important questions worthy of exploring during quiet alone-time, along with a more central query: "What does intimacy feel like?"

Let's define intimacy as a close relationship that resonates, for both individuals, from deep within, while at the same time affording each person the willingness to be influenced, mirrored, or changed by the other's reality. A sense of enthusiasm and "full-aliveness" appears to derive from a rare and uncanny sense of being mutually in tune with one another. In such moments, we feel as though we *transcend* our differences with another person, while we also *assert* and *accept* those differences. Such an experience holds the potential for adding a new depth of intimacy to any relationship. One may ask, "What could possibly be more intimate and healing than to have a sense of abiding connection, of companionship, with another being that is based on exactly this kind of deep, mutually shared understanding, empathy, and collaboration?" The only plausible answer I can think of is, "Having that same level of intimacy with your self."

Balancing intimacy and solitude within any relationship is not easy. It can be one of the most difficult tasks in an intimate bond between two people. As described earlier, part of this has to do with the ambivalent or negative feelings that may be directed toward the person who actively chooses to spend some quiet time alone. Despite our professed tolerance for individual expression and the celebration of personal freedom, there is a constant push toward conformity. Rocking the boat is not long tolerated by most passengers. The person who rebels or deviates may be labeled anti-social, eccentric, or downright hostile. Choosing to move away physically may be interpreted as a deliberate decision to separate emotionally, engendering feelings of rejection and devaluation, particularly in our relationship with an intimate companion.

If a person's temporary immersion in silence and solitude is from a loved one—such as a wife, husband, or partner—the person left behind may experience feelings of mistrust, abandonment, suspicion, guilt, anger, or envy. The person may ask, "What is wrong with me?" or, "Why don't you want to be with me?" This is understandable if there's a fundamental difference in desire or attitude regarding solitude. The person who withdraws must exercise tact and sensitivity when reacting to such expressions, since the loved one left behind is likely to feel vulnerable and uncertain.

Journalist Cheryl Jarvis addressed the rejection issue when she described the premeditated "time outs" taken by fifty-five contemporary women (including herself) in *The Marriage Sabbatical: The Journey That Brings You Home.* In researching her book, Jarvis conducted a random survey of American women, most of them under age forty-five, who had deliberately taken time away from their husbands and children in order to find more balance in their lives.

Virtually all the women described in *The Marriage Sabbatical* viewed their embrace of personal alone-time as a means of sharpening a sense of themselves as distinct individuals, separated from family members while still feeling connected to them. In one passage, the author's husband, Jim, confessed his deepest fear: "You think, 'Gee, maybe she'll like being away so much that she won't want to come back.'" What Jarvis found through her research, however, was that each of the women returned from her personal retreat to find that loved ones managed better than they had expected, which eased guilt and boosted confidence all around. In the end, the women felt more intimately linked to their husbands and children as a result of being alone.

"[The wives discovered that] they can extricate themselves from everyone and nothing falls apart," reported Jarvis. Exploring the same theme, a less formal survey of married women conducted by Marjorie Williams and reported in the February 2001 issue of *Talk* magazine came up with similar results. Wrote Williams in summation: "I have come to believe that even in the best of marriages, in the most devoted of mothers, there lurks a thirst for solitude."

The conclusions reached by Jarvis and Williams spur the question, "How much do we use our ties to spouse or family as a reason *not* to find a separate time and space for ourselves?" Both women and men might find a positive role model in Depression-era aviator Amelia Earhart, who, according to Barbara Holland in *One's Company*, spent a month away from her husband each year so that she could teach at Purdue University. Other disappearances, of shorter duration, were standard fare in the couple's unorthodox relationship. "I may have to keep some place where I can go to be myself now and then," the famous pilot wrote her groom at the time of their marriage. "I cannot guarantee to endure at all times the confinements of even an attractive cage."

The decision to take some time in silence and solitude underscores the fact that there *are* limits to intimacy, that each one of us is, ultimately and irrevocably, alone in this world. Confronting this existential truth requires not only that we accept our inability to be "all things" even to those we love most, but that our first allegiance is to understanding (and following) our own route to happiness, which may sometimes exclude those with whom we feel the deepest love and greatest level of intimacy.

As we mature, many of us come to understand that the most satisfying intimate relationships do not demand that we merge completely with another human—making him or her the "be-all and end-all" of our existence—but that we establish an equilibrium between our simultaneous yearning for intimate connection and self-fulfilling independence. This acceptance of our simultaneous intertwining and separateness is part of what makes us fully human, able and willing to give to and receive from others in a loving and intimate way. Our embrace of silence and solitude—taking time to observe and accept our imperfections as well as our joys and successes—helps us welcome those same aspects of others through compassion and empathy that is born of self-love rather than a sense of obligation or duty.

The exploration of quiet alone-time opens the hearts of many people who let nondoing and stillness speak to them. Instead of evaluating their experience through intellect, they may consider other perspectives that are less "left-brain." An embrace of silence and solitude on an ongoing basis may gradually help us place more trust in our own interior voice: call it intuition, gut instinct, or "right brain" insight. The opinions of others, along with cultural imperatives and contemporary thinking, may fade in importance and influence. We may grow to know more about who we are and what serves us best by picking and choosing from what is available as well as by seeking out new resources.

The Thai spiritual leader, Achaan Chah, assured his students that, in silence and solitude, "you will reach a point where the heart tells itself what to do." In our quiet alone-time, the striving of the rational mind to shape and control intimacy may subside as the intellect yields to wisdom from other dimensions of mind and spirit.

These changes in perspective regarding self may signal a shift in other relationships: to family, to work, to community, and to specific spiritual traditions or religious practices. As a direct result of our muted contemplation, we may decide the way we approach and respond to life is, in important ways, not meeting our needs and desires.

For example, the practice of stopping each day to experience silence and solitude may lead us to conclude that we are not living in a suitable physical environment. If we live in a big city, our tolerance for the high noise level to which we were once oblivious may have evaporated. The frenetic pace of urban life, which perhaps once served to stimulate us in a pleasurable way, may have become intolerable. Peace and quiet may have become such a high priority that we are willing to quit our job, uproot our family, and relocate to a less crowded city, to a village, or a rural area. Thousands of people do this each year, for this very reason.

Newfound sensitivities can be hard to deny. During my thirties, before I made it a regular practice to seek out silence and solitude, I lived in the scruffy Venice district of Los Angeles. Many years later, I can still close my eyes and hear the buzzing of police helicopters, the hum of the Santa Monica Freeway, and the wail of sirens along Lincoln Avenue. In an instant, I can resurrect the whining of leaf-blowers, the barking of dogs, the thumping of rap music, and the honking of horns. Obviously, I did—

and still could, if necessary—adjust to this cacophony. But I prefer not to do so, which is one of the reasons I now live in a small city in an under-populated Western state.

Other priorities may assert themselves as your attentive awareness brings into focus present realities and possible alternatives. I have a friend in Washington, D.C., whose entire relationship with work began to change after she regularly sat in silence and subsequently determined that, without question, she needed to find a job that reflected her social values. At the time, Chris worked for a small company whose owners were very conservative and whose services promoted their political agenda aggressively. My friend had always been disturbed by this, since her own views were at the opposite end of the spectrum. Still, she considered hers a good job and stuck with it because the position offered some unusual benefits, including the chance to work flexible hours. Eventually, Chris attended night school and developed new skills that led her to a more satisfying job as a fundraiser for a politically progressive nonprofit group. Chris now earns less money, but is much happier.

The insights wrought by quiet alone-time can prompt dramatic realignments in intimate personal relationships, too. I once met a man who, through a series of solo retreats, realized how distant he was from his wife and young children. Peter's demanding, hard-charging job for a Boston real estate firm had magnified his competitive impulses to the point where he was unable to relate to his passive wife as an equal, or to soften his harsh interactions with his kids. Peter had become a stranger to them, and to himself. Within a year after experiencing this epiphany, he had changed jobs, moved to a farm in another state, and reforged loving relationships with members of his family again.

For others, an inspiration to lead a kinder and more compassionate life may pull them into part-time or full-time volunteerism or paid service work. One might think of this as a way of *living* your values instead of mouthing them. As the expression goes, "You need to walk your talk." I am reminded of President Jimmy Carter, who has described the influence prayer and meditation has on his commitment to do humanitarian work: building Habitat for Humanity houses, monitoring elections in developing countries, drawing attention to preventable health emergencies, and being a vocal champion of human rights. Perhaps Carter was favorably influenced by his mother, Lillian, who served happily in the Peace Corps while in her sixties, and by his early life as a farmer, an occupation that demands both patience and faith.

Kindness and compassion may emerge from quiet alone-time as qualities that can help us to understand the life-decisions that others have
made, or to place such decisions in a new context. An embrace of silence
and solitude may even help many of us who are on our own, with or
without children, to cope with feelings of loneliness and social estrangement in a society oriented primarily toward heterosexual couples and
their families.

Humans differ in temperament and predilection, of course, which
helps explain how each of us can react so differently to the prospect of
extended solitude and silence. People also vary in how much they value
personal relationships. Some are almost phobic in their fear of being
alone, while others are content to become—by society's accounting—
lone wolves, solitaires, and oddballs. Still others fit the definition of what
writer Sasha Cagen dubbed "quirkyalones" in a 2000 *Utne Reader* magazine article.

Describing herself as "deeply single" and "almost never in a [roman-
tic] relationship," Cagen wrote that she and her fellow quirkyalones "are
the puzzle pieces who seldom fit with other puzzle pieces. . . . We inhabit
singledom as our natural resting state. In a world where proms and marriages define the social order, we are, by force of our personalities and
inner strengths, rebels."

While Cagen's quirkyalones are open to having intimate relationships, they feel fine without them. Friends and family help sustain them,
but they also regard being alone "as a wellspring of feeling and experience. There is a bittersweet fondness for silence," declares Cagen. "All
those nights alone—they bring insight." In the still quiet, a better understanding of self (and others) evolves naturally.

The patron saint of this group, which Cagen puts at less than 5 percent of the population, may be Rainer Maria Rilke, the German poet
who advised: "Your solitude will be a hold and home for you even amid
very unfamiliar conditions and from there you will find all your ways."
Rilke recognized that, for some people, there is safety and familiarity in
aloneness. Avoiding intimacy, he implied, may be a way of avoiding risk,
but it also allows more energy to be directed toward deeper intimacy
with self. For some, the latter is more fulfilling as well as a requirement
for deep intimacy with a loved one.

At least some quirkyalones are what Abraham Maslow labeled "cre-
atives." The pioneering psychologist defined members of this group as

individuals who actualize themselves with little apparent need for others. Such an inspired person, wrote Maslow in *The Farther Reaches of Human Nature,* often "loses his past and future and lives only in the moment. He is totally immersed, fascinated, and absorbed." In fact, "this ability to become 'lost in the present' seems to be a sine qua non for creativeness of any kind. But also certain prerequisites of creativeness—in whatever realm—somehow have something to do with this ability to become timeless, selfless, [and] outside of space, of society, of history."

For the artist, poet, composer, philosopher, photographer, or writer, the sparks of inspiration and fire of creativity often are born in solitude. Quiet alone-time may be essential not only to their professions but to their basic well-being. Anthony Storr has noted that "many creative activities are predominantly solitary. [Such actions] are concerned with self-realization and self-development in isolation, or with finding some coherent pattern in life. The degree to which these creative activities take priority in the life of the individual varies with his personality and talents. Everyone needs some human relationships; but everyone also needs some kind of fulfillment which is relevant to himself alone."

Storr points out that while most of us develop and mature primarily through our interactions and roles relative to others, the singularly creative person "is able to mature primarily on his own. His passage through life is defined by the changing nature and increasing maturity of his work."

While these states may be the crucible in which creative expression ignites and burns, they may also represent a way out for those who, like quirkyalones, are intensely aware that they do not fit into society's mainstream. Withdrawal may seem a better choice than enduring social situations that feel uncomfortable, perhaps because of perceived differences in interests and values or as a result of past traumas involving loss, ridicule, and rejection. Such a person may prefer to choose the familiar warm blanket of solitude rather than the cool emotional uncertainty of interaction with others. For some quirkyalones, spending a lot of time alone prompts them to spend even *more* time alone, potentially triggering an unhealthy cycle of closeness and withdrawal. As in all natural systems, a return to balance is the route to good health.

Mindfulness can help restore us to balance and, more than that, bring forth creative expression from places that are dark, painful, and greatly feared. Without unlocking the doors to such places, we may expend great energy over the course of a lifetime in trying to keep them closed.

Through a cathartic process of self-discovery, we may be healed and born anew, as impressionable and intuitive as a small child.

Over the course of my many weeks alone, shifting reactions to silence and solitude were reflected in the entries of my journal.

FEBRUARY 8—DAY 21

Clouds and light snow almost all day. I don't like these "indoor days" and I am grouchy. The house gets cold and I need to keep the fire going, but I miss the friendly warmth of the sun. I get tired of my limited choices: reading, writing (by hand, since the solar panel won't power the computer on cloudy days), cooking, eating, listening to the radio, listening to tapes, practicing yoga, and drawing. It all feels too passive. Cabin fever. I am looking forward to hiking, instead of always strapping on snowshoes or skis. There are days when I don't want to do either one.

I am irritable today. Probably I wouldn't feel so strongly except that the snowfall is very light, almost incidental. It would be one thing to have two snowy days that yielded six or eight inches, but this entire white weekend has brought two inches at the most. How I want things to be different than they are!

Saki Santorelli, director of the Stress Reduction Center founded by Jon Kabat-Zinn at the University of Massachusetts, cautions in *Heal Thy Self* that if we refuse to take this journey to our wounded places—and each of us has them—"we may never play the music of our own lives. We might never sing the song that is only ours to sing. What a tragedy this would be." In silence and solitude the waiting world is infinitely patient, eager to hear the voices that are ours alone.

I have taken these kinds of bittersweet journeys several times as part of extended meditation retreats as well as during my fourteen weeks in the wilderness. I recall how, in 1991, during my first week-long silent meditation retreat in the mountains of northern New Mexico, my mind vigorously resisted settling into the regimentation of a strict timetable. The orderly routine of such gatherings invariably includes alternating periods of sitting and walking meditation, as well as specific times for meals, communal work, meeting with teachers, and listening to "dharma talks" (lectures on philosophical and spiritual topics).

By the end of the second day, I confronted one of my dark and painful sides: the tight anger and panic-filled claustrophobia I experienced when confined by either a restrictive schedule or a crowded physical space.

Even in childhood, personal freedom promised an escape from what felt like intolerably oppressive situations at home and in school. I am sure this has been a factor in my choice to spend most of my adult life as a freelance writer, fashioning a flexible schedule and working at home under conditions of my own choosing.

"I keep having to resist the impulse to get up and walk out of the meditation hall," I told Jack Kornfield, my teacher, who trained in Thailand as a Buddhist monk. "When we are told what to do, I automatically want to do the opposite."

Jack looked at me impassively and assessed the frustrated expression on my face.

"So what's the problem?" he asked, with a shrug of his shoulders.

"This regimentation is exactly the opposite of the way I lead my life at home and in my work," I said. "It feels artificial to sit when I don't necessarily want to sit, or to walk when I don't feel the desire to walk. Why can't I meditate on my own terms, when the conditions feel right to me and when I think it would do me the most good?"

Jack smiled and his brown eyes twinkled mischievously. "You already know the answer to that question. This is where your work is, at least for this time and in this place. Look at your eagerness to run away and learn what that powerful impulse of mind and emotion has to teach you."

I stayed for the rest of the week. Although I cannot honestly say that I felt happy about the limits imposed by the retreat's schedule, I came to accept them. My resistance to structure and control is still a personal issue I work on, and perhaps always will.

Whatever you consider your ongoing personal issues to be, they are bound to include aspects of independence and intimacy. As humans, we dance constantly between poles of desire and rejection. Sometimes we embrace those we love, both literally and figuratively, as a way of feeling connected. At other moments we embrace only ourselves, seeking a kind of closeness with self that even our loved ones occasionally inhibit. Through quiet alone-time, we come to accept that we need not remain at either extreme. Striking a healthy equilibrium is the goal, and it is best achieved by tuning in regularly to the inner voices that external voices often obscure.

CHAPTER NINE

NATURE'S SILENCE AND SOLITUDE

The stillness of the wilderness imposes itself
with an enveloping hush; a visitor has little choice
but to be internally quiet as well.

—David Douglas, *Wilderness Sojourn:
Notes in the Desert Silence*

What is the greatest length of time you have ever spent alone, physically apart from other humans?" Long-time Sierra Club president and staunch environmentalist David Brower made a practice of posing this question to people he encountered. Few could say they had ever been by themselves for more than twenty-four hours. Many had never spent as long as half a day on their own.

The late conservationist found responses to his question instructive because they shed light on the issue closest to his heart: how to preserve the Earth's fast-disappearing wilderness. The fact that most people had spent no significant time alone underscored for Brower the difficulty of convincing them that there was exquisite grace and priceless value in preserving the natural silence and solitude of a pristine environment. He reasoned that if his fellow humans had no experience of being quiet and alone, they might not support actions that would limit noise pollution, road building, access by motorized vehicles, and the use of firearms on our most fragile and threatened public lands.

Brower's loaded question raises underlying issues that are vital and urgent. Solitude is vanishing not only from our wildest places but also from our homes, yards, suburbs, and farmlands. Even our national parks are not immune. Increasingly, those who seek contemplative peace and soothing quiet in nature must deal with the noise rendered by airplanes, helicopters, off-road vehicles, boats, portable radios, and, in some areas, the tinkling bells that hikers wear to scare away bears.

We are in danger of losing something truly precious before we appreciate its capacity to soothe, restore, and enlighten. Statistics confirm that, throughout the world, open space is being lost to development many times faster than parks are being created. At the same time, those who manage our natural resources are forced to open ever-larger areas to those whose preferred forms of recreation make noise, such as all-terrain driving, powerboating, and snowmobiling.

For now, thankfully, a great deal of the natural world remains mostly untrammeled, particularly in the western United States, Alaska, and Canada. These lands continue to be a resource for those who seek high-quality solitude in the outdoors, even if the silence is no longer absolute.

Several spiritual traditions incorporate a respect for quiet alone-time in nature. Appreciation and care for the environment play a central role in Taoism, a religious doctrine that originated in ancient China and is now followed by millions of people throughout the world. Taoists advocate a life of simplicity and noninterference with natural events. By living in harmony with the Tao (the way of nature), it is believed that happiness and enlightenment may be found.

One of Taoism's founding philosophers, the Chinese sage Lao-Tzu, knew the value of such a refuge 2,600 years ago when he urged his peers to remove themselves from the pressures of human society and savor the healing influence of the natural world. "Express yourself completely, then be quiet," he advised in the *Tao Te Ching,* his classic manual for living. "Be like the forces of nature: when it blows, there is only wind; when it rains, there is only rain; when the clouds pass, the sun shines through." Later, Lao-Tzu observed that "the master makes use of [silence and solitude], embracing his aloneness [and] realizing he is one with the whole universe."

Such a restorative place can be as close as our own backyard. Or, for apartment and city-dwellers, as accessible as the public park down the street. For those who have the time and means to travel, nature's greatest gifts may be found in a wilder and vaster locale a bit farther away. With a little time and money, we can get to such a destination by car, train, bus, or airplane.

Some of us are fortunate to develop a special relationship with a particular place that, along with great beauty, offers exceptional silence and solitude. A prime example is the Sonoran Desert of southwestern Arizona, which has remained largely uninhabited and undeveloped throughout human history.

Tucson-based writer Charles Bowden is one of a growing number of people campaigning to create a national park in this empty quarter, insisting that its vast wilderness of rocks and cacti comprises, in Bowden's opinion, "the last stronghold in our nation for silence." In a December 1999 *Esquire* article, "Leave Society Behind," Bowden says that the Sonoran Desert is "the one place where we can finally hear ourselves," with "a level of quiet the cemeteries only hear about by rumor." The five-thousand-square-mile tract south of Phoenix, he continues, is "a country where we hear the breath of life." For Bowden and others who know the transformative power of such a stunning environment, the Sonoran is worth preserving for reasons beyond its spectacular beauty

QUIET ALONE-TIME IN NATURE

A 1999 opinion survey by the Luntz organization confirmed that most Americans harbor positive feelings about the value of the outdoors as a place to relax and rejuvenate.

- More than one-half of those polled cited an outdoor location, such as a park, wilderness area, or beach, as their preferred place to vacation.

- Eighty-five percent of people surveyed thought "parks and open space contribute to property values and [the] economic stability of neighborhoods."

- When asked, nine out of ten Americans agreed that "park, recreation, and conservation programs provide places for children to learn skills and values such as teamwork and respect for nature. Three in four believe such programs help prevent juvenile delinquency.

- One-third of respondents said they preferred using a government budget surplus for parks and open space rather than on tax cuts.

Source: *Americans for Our Heritage and Recreation, 1999 Luntz Poll*

and more prosaic recreational opportunities.

Having camped there, I can assure you that the silence of the Sonoran Desert is deafening, except for the low-flying U.S. Border Patrol and Air Force planes that punctuate its solitude. But apart from its extreme harshness, the Sonoran is not so different from other places where humans are absent. Indeed, silence is the norm in nature. We have become oblivious to this background of silence because we have covered it with layers of our own noise.

The potential exists for plenty of loud sound in the natural world—from roaring hurricanes to laughing hyenas—yet things are quiet in most environments most of the time. Subtract the rustlings caused by wind or the vocalizations of birds and the world is even more quiet.

The majority of aural vibrations that surround us are human made, which becomes obvious when we close our eyes and pay close attention to what we hear: automobile motors, airplanes, telephones, computers, clocks, voices, and all manner of machinery. A hopeful implication of this sobering reality is that we retain much of the power to create silent conditions in our lives, simply by shutting off (or out) unwanted sound. We may even be drawn to do this by something basic in our nature.

Anthropologist Joan Halifax describes a human craving for quiet alone-time in *The Fruitful Darkness,* her study of the mind's need for connection and balance. Halifax sees the embrace of silence and solitude as an affirmation that a psychic world beyond and predating technology continues to shape our experience. "There is a difference," Halifax wrote, "in a life that is lived on the level of the universal or general and one that is lived through the experience of detail and with the sense of the particularly strong present. We need to do this in order to acknowledge fully and completely our biological and physical world, and how our social institutions and personal views shape our lives and our planet. [Yet] industrial cultures have rejected the biological, the earthly."

One danger of living without this sense of connection to nature—writer Ruth Baetz calls it "communion"—is the risk of reacting to events *only* through our limited human perspective when no other means of relating is accessible. Those who live in cities, for example, move through physical spaces shaped by their fellow humans, reflecting a people-biased perception of the world. Here the hand of artifice is felt everywhere.

Halifax recalls how, listening to the high-pitched song of crickets on hot summer nights in rural California, she often thought "of the impoverishment of being born and dying in New York or Mexico City, where these songs are not heard. I can no longer deny the consequences of living in a world where the humming of machines, not crickets, forms the auditory background of our dreams."

For urbanites, whose ties to nature are problematic, an escape to the countryside may prove a powerful, healing antidote to the unrelenting presence of harsh mechanical sounds. City-bound parents surely realize this when they send their children to summer camp—and themselves on getaways to tropical islands.

Colorado-based writer John A. Murray, in *The Quotable Nature Lover,* believes we should maintain a refuge as a personal getaway, even if it is only a favorite hiking trail, city park, or public beach. Such a sanctuary

NATURE AS THERAPY

The therapeutic benefits of interacting with the natural world are well-documented. In 1997, for example, the *Mind/Body Health Newsletter* reported that "overall job satisfaction appears to be significantly higher among workers with a view of nature. A major survey found that those able to look out on nature scenes also report significantly fewer medical ailments than their viewless co-workers." The study went on to suggest that a view of nature from one's hospital window "can contribute more to recovery from surgery than many drugs."

Harvard-trained physician Bill Thomas, the medical director of several New England nursing homes, has written about nature's impact on health, commenting on the enormous success of getting patients connected with plants. In a conversation detailed in our book *Tending the Earth, Mending the Spirit,* Thomas told my colleague, Connie Goldman, that in nature-deprived facilities, "we found terrible loneliness caused by a lack of companionship, a lack of opportunity to give care, and a high incidence of boredom."

When hospitals add plants to private rooms, public spaces, and windows, patients responded dramatically. At the first nursing home where Thomas made such changes, rates of infection and drug prescription were cut in half. Death rates dropped 15 percent the first year, 25 percent the second. Subsequent clinical and academic studies concluded that "horticulture therapy" may be an effective way to lower blood pressure, slow bone loss, improve circulation, reduce stress, soothe anxiety, and stimulate the brain.

"If you think about it," Thomas told Connie, "people all over the world go to great lengths to put themselves in natural surroundings. Parks, for instance, are a terrific relief valve for an overly humanized environment. There is a huge need for this kind of contact."

allows us "figuratively, if not literally, to suspend membership in the human race." U. S. presidents have always known the value of refuge, Murray points out, citing a parade of retreats ranging from George Washington's Mt. Vernon and Thomas Jefferson's Monticello to the Martha's Vineyard compound of Bill Clinton and the Texas ranch of George W. Bush.

From a biological point of view, our presidents are doing what comes naturally to most mammal species. A basic part of our animal nature is the occasional craving for withdrawal. Many of our fellow mammals, including cats and bears, lead solitary lives. They get together to mate or raise families before embarking on their own again. In contrast, humans often socialize with other humans when offered the choice. We are gregarious creatures in both temperament and habit. Billions of us live in cities, and even when we live in rural areas, we group ourselves in towns and villages. Throughout the world, it is easier to be with people than away from them, to be immersed in human-made sound rather than isolated from it. On every inhabited continent, the trend is toward more urbanization, not less.

Sometimes humans go to extremes to experience silence and solitude. Indeed, sometimes our thirst for adventure can lead us to some of the most quiet places on Earth. When someone undertakes immersion in extremes of solitude in the great outdoors, the results can be particularly instructive. In *Solitude: A Return to the Self,* Anthony Storr cites U. S. Navy admiral Robert E. Byrd is an unusual yet relevant example. The polar explorer, who had previously described himself as extraordinarily happy in his private life, spent the winter of 1934 alone in Antarctica, which was at that time a terribly isolated continent with none of the modern amenities enjoyed by those stationed there today.

Byrd later reflected on the five bitterly cold months he endured in near-constant darkness. "I had no important purposes," he wrote, "except one man's desire to know that kind of experience to the full; to be by himself for a while and to taste peace and quiet and solitude long enough to find out how good they really are."

The change in outlook wrought by this solitary season had a deep impact on the explorer. Four years after his return, Byrd concluded he had gained something: "An appreciation of the sheer miracle and beauty of being alive, and a humble set of values." Being back in civilization had altered his essential ideas about life. "I live more simply now," the then-retired admiral mused, "and with more peace."

Such experiences are not the exclusive province of stalwart individuals like Admiral Byrd. They are within the grasp of each of us. Even lives that seem ordinary can be powerfully linked to the extraordinary silence and solitude (and intriguing mysteries) of nature.

As a boy growing up on the edge of a small town in northern California, I felt magic and excitement when I roamed beyond the fence lines. I knew that the nearby meadows, creeks, hills, and mountains were special as well to my parents, who had bought their home in part because they considered it a terrific place to raise their five kids. It seemed that all of the other children—and parents—in my neighborhood loved their proximity to nature as much as we did. Ours was a stereotype of the suburban California lifestyle, with as much time spent outdoors as possible.

My parents owned a big house on a small lot, filling almost every inch of their quarter-acre with trees, shrubs, and flowers. I was encouraged to grow a vegetable garden and, with my brothers, to harvest walnuts from the trees a previous owner, a farmer, had planted. Less than a hundred yards away a creek meandered, its banks a thick jungle of riparian vegetation. The lazy stream was home to fish, turtles, frogs, toads, and snails. Along its route lurked salamanders, raccoons, skunks, snakes, and squirrels, not to mention dozens of species of birds and butterflies. When I tired of this lush habitat, there were always the oak-studded hills, where my dog and I would flush deer from thickets and scare mice out of rotting stumps. Mountain lions and bobcats prowled unseen beneath the cover of night.

On weekend trips to visit aunts and cousins, our family would drive past naturalist John Muir's then-abandoned Martinez home, now a national historic park. As a teenager, I followed Muir's admonition to "climb the mountains and get their good tidings." When I went backpacking in his beloved Sierra Nevada, I knew exactly what the pioneering environmental activist referred to in this journal entry found in *The Quotable Nature Lover:* "When I first came down to the city from my mountain home, I began to wither, and to wish instinctively for the vital woods and high sky."

A deep and abiding connection to nature is something with which many of us can identify, even if our entire lives are spent in cities or suburbia. This is why urbanites take the trouble to create city parks, which cost money and often fly in the face of extreme development pressures. Somehow, everyone agrees that parks are a simple necessity, like clean water and good food. Imagine New Yorkers auctioning off Central Park to the highest bidder. It will never happen. The people of Manhattan are sustained by their huge, tree-shaded swath of green.

WHERE TO FIND THE SILENCE AND SOLITUDE OF NATURE

Take a few minutes to consider natural environments in which you would like to spend time (or perhaps already visit). Write down the names of such places and keep the list where you can refer to it easily. A good reference point is a page in your personal journal or a sheet of paper stuck to your refrigerator. Here are a few possible entries:

• *Your own backyard, or someone else's.*

• *A park, playground, or zoo within easy walking or driving distance.*

• *A neighborhood garden.*

• *A green belt or open space on the outskirts of your community.*

• *A church, college, or university that has landscaped grounds or other outdoor areas that are open to the public.*

• *A path along a lake, river, canal, or stream.*

• *A beach.*

• *A cottage or other dwelling in the country that's available to you.*

• *If you live in a multiunit building, a garden, balcony, or rooftop space exposed to the sky and breeze.*

While writing this book, I was interviewed by Kathryn Rem, a reporter for the Illinois newspaper *Springfield State Journal,* who was interested in the subject of silence and solitude. Within a few days of talking to me by telephone, Rem was surprised by the number of people she encountered, chosen at random, who sought time in nature as an antidote to their noisy, busy lives.

"Susan Nelson likes to sit in the shade of her backyard dogwood tree and enjoy the beauty and fresh air," Rem wrote in an article about quiet alone-time. "Todd Withcomb, a student, spends his Saturdays hiking or biking in a city park or hunting for mushrooms. . . . [Office worker] Yvonne Bronke is an avid gardener who revels in the loveliness and silence of her yard." Said Bronke: "'I make time for myself and my dog; it's so peaceful here, listening to the water garden and the frogs.'"

Nearly two thousand miles west of Illinois, the officials who run Zion National Park in southern Utah discovered park visitors felt much the same desire for solace and sanctuary. In May 2000, administrators began providing tourists who arrive during Zion's peak months with propane-powered buses instead of allowing them to drive through the park in their own vehicles.

Visitors now talk enthusiastically about the quiet that envelopes them as soon as they step off the shuttles that take them to viewpoints along six-mile Zion Scenic Drive. The silence is a fringe benefit of the ban on cars, invoked as a response to parking shortages and traffic jams that were frustrating visitors, injuring wildlife, and increasing air pollution.

"After their first ride, I've had people who've been coming to Zion for years say that they feel like they've never been here before," Shirley Ballard, co-owner of a local motel, told a reporter for Colorado-based *High Country News*. "There's no buses idling in a cloud of diesel fumes and no RVs with generators. It's amazing." The 85 percent initial public approval rating for the car-free Zion was so high that similar public transportation systems have been implemented in other heavily visited national parks.

To be sure, Zion tourists are not experiencing a completely quiet and empty place. But instead of car alarms, motor-home air conditioners, and idling engines, they are now able to hear what once was obliterated: the gentle murmur of the Virgin River, the lonely croak of a spade-foot toad, and the cascading trill of a canyon wren. Visitors now admire the wonders of nature through every sense, including that of hearing.

HOW DO YOU LIKE TO EXPERIENCE NATURE?

Make a list of the particular aspects of the natural world that help you feel more at ease. Ask yourself, "When was the last time I felt soothed and restored by nature—and why?" Everyone's list will be different, but here are some choices that may resonate with you, or at least prompt a fond memory:

- *The cathedral-like majesty of a grove of mature trees, as in a long-established park or an old-growth forest.*

- *The hypnotic crash and fall of surf on a beach, advancing and retreating with the tide.*

- *The sight of birds outside your window: singing, courting, building nests, gathering food, or teaching their fledglings to fly.*

- *The tingling brace of a cool wind blowing away a heat wave or signaling the approach of a storm front.*

- *The sensory pleasure of seeing spring flowers in bloom, autumn leaves showing off their bright colors, or trees bearing summer fruit.*

For many, a direct experience of the natural world is the easiest and most dependable way to connect quickly with silence and solitude. This may partially explain why gardening is such a popular leisure activity in the United States, Canada, and much of Europe. We crave interaction with nature, even if it's limited to nurturing a single houseplant or growing tomatoes on a narrow apartment balcony. It is almost as though our instincts guide us toward this activity, in the same way that hidden processes stir the migration impulse in birds or prompt bears to put on weight for their winter hibernation.

"The natural environment has turned out to be the most powerful setting to reduce mental fatigue we've found," declared Steven Kaplan, a University of Michigan environmental psychologist, in a 1994 *McCall's* magazine interview. The brain, Kaplan has shown, responds to nature in a variety of positive ways that can be measured. But maybe no further explanation of our craving is really necessary: when our brains get tired, they follow an innate urge to rest and recharge themselves in the serenity of the outdoors.

New Mexico writer David Douglas acknowledged as much in his book, *Wilderness Sojourn: Notes in the Desert Silence.* The natural world "strips away that disguise [of civilization] and leaves me and my strivings exposed," Douglas confessed. "When I am at home, in the city, I complain about distractions, yet surround myself with them: magazines, radio, newspapers, television. Hungry for news and entertainment, I often fill to overflowing the spaces of silence. . . . Elsewhere a frenetic pace enables me to camouflage myself; by staying busy I don't have time to evaluate my pursuits."

THREE PERSPECTIVES ON
QUIET ALONE-TIME IN WILD PLACES

For generations, American writers have celebrated the silence and solitude of their country's natural environment. Here is a sampling.

- Wallace Stegner, from *Wilderness Letter:* "Something will have gone out of us as a people if we ever let the remaining wilderness be destroyed." Access to wilderness is "the thing that has helped to make an American different from, and, until we forget it in the roar of our industrial cities, more fortunate than other men. For an American, insofar as he is new and different at all, is a civilized man who has renewed himself in the wild."

- John Burroughs, from *Pepacton:* "The mood in which you set out on a spring or autumn ramble or a sturdy winter walk . . . is the mood in which your best thoughts and impulses come to you, or in which you might embark on any heroic or noble enterprise. Life is sweet in such moments, the universe is complete, and there is no failure or imperfection anywhere."

- Mark Twain, from *Roughing It:* "It was a superb summer morning and all the landscape was brilliant with sunshine. There was a freshness and a breeziness, too, and an exhilarating sense of emancipation from all sorts of cares and responsibilities that made us feel that the years we had spent in the close, hot city, toiling and slaving, had been wasted and thrown away."

For Douglas, a day or two spent camping in the American West allows the stillness of nature to impose itself on his "frenetic pace" with a comforting hush. "A visitor has little choice," he notes, "but to be internally quiet as well."

Utah writer and environmentalist Terry Tempest Williams takes this notion a step further. She believes that "some lands are truly special" not only because of how they look or what distinctive life-forms flourish there, but "because of the spiritual values they hold for society and for what they inspire: silence, awe, beauty, majesty." This conviction informs Williams's ardent activism, which seeks to preserve at least some remote but threatened wilderness areas so that future generations will have a few more places to escape the din of urban life and the tyranny of technology.

Those of us who live in North America are fortunate to inhabit a continent that still boasts considerable open space, as compared to Europe, Southeast Asia, and other crowded regions. Knowing this, I am not surprised by how many Western Europeans and Japanese, for example, are drawn each year to the expansive high desert landscape of the southwestern United States, where I have lived since 1988. Often the minds of these visitors are boggled—and their hearts stirred—by the simple majesty of so much unadulterated nature. I have met foreigners who marvel that a fifty-mile view does not encompass a single building or road. The idea of unencumbered silence and spaciousness is a complete novelty.

Most of us don't have to travel far to set the stage for such an epiphany. It is available to us almost everywhere we go, if we merely open our eyes to the everyday miracles of the natural world. An example from my own experience took place far from my beloved New Mexico. While on a Midwestern outing near the village of Alma, Wisconsin, I climbed to the top of a bluff that afforded a magnificent view of the upper Mississippi River. A bald eagle was soaring above the broad river's lush adjacent wetlands, while a fox trotted through the flood plains on his hunting circuit. Affixed to a boulder at my feet was a weathered plaque that bore this sentimental yet accurate message: "Such scenes have the power to quiet the restless pulse of care." I urge you to seek such places with a passion. I assure you, they lie in wait of your discovery wherever you are.

SIMPLE WAYS TO ENJOY THE QUIET SOUNDS OF NATURE

How easy is it to embrace the natural quiet of the outdoors? How readily can we disconnect from the clamor of civilization? The opportunities are limitless, but here are a few suggestions:

- *Get up at dawn, when birds and other animals are most active and the workaday world is at its lowest ebb.*

- *Spend time each month in a natural environment (such as a park) that has few human-made sounds or where nature's sounds are louder than those of humans or machines. These might include a seashore, an arboretum, or a bird sanctuary.*

- *Place a small decorative water fountain in your living space or yard. An outdoor fountain attracts birds and the sound of cascading water indoors is relaxing. Small fountains that recycle water through a quiet pump are widely available.*

- *As a comforting background, play a CD or tape of environmental sounds. Recordings are available from such idyllic locations as forested mountains, empty beaches, gargling streams, and grassy meadows. The sounds of whales, dolphins, and birds are other popular choices.*

The voices of nature speak in life-affirming ways. Such sounds can be liberating, inspiring, and spiritually uplifting. They have the capacity to teach us important lessons not just about the outdoors but about our innermost selves.

In his poetic book, *The Outermost House,* Henry Beston reflected on the few years he spent living alone among the sand dunes and sea creatures of the eastern beaches of Cape Cod during the 1920s. He had limited interaction with his distant neighbors, but found his intimate contact with the natural world a way of connecting with something primeval—and immensely satisfying. "I lived as a solitary, yes, but I made no pretense of acting the conventional hermit," Beston wrote. "I lived in the midst of an abundance of natural life which manifested itself every hour of the day, and from being thus surrounded, thus enclosed within a great whirl of what one might call 'the life force,' I felt that I drew a secret and sustaining energy. There were times, on the threshold of spring, when the force seemed as real as heat from the sun. . . . Life is as much a force in the universe as electricity or gravitational pull, and the presence of life sustains life."

Since childhood, I have felt a similar draw toward the outdoors. I am always at home in nature, filled with deep serenity and a gentle sensation of connectedness. The outdoors teaches me lessons I desperately need, whether comforting or painful, and other times I almost feel myself merging with the landscape in something that approaches ecstatic bliss. Part of the excitement of exploring nature is discovering what will happen, which may be nothing in particular on any given day. Most of the time, however, there is at least one encounter that surprises and delights or challenges and confronts. And then there are those rare occasions when, as Annie Dillard describes in *Pilgrim at Tinker Creek,* the emergent insight from this quiet alone-time "rocks and topples you; it will shear, loose, launch, winnow, and grind."

Kentucky farmer and essayist Wendell Berry, like Dillard, describes the transformative power of nature. When he walks through the woods near his home, the essentials of life seem to align themselves effortlessly. "I enter an order that does not exist outside, in the human spaces," Berry wrote in *Native Hill*. "I feel my life take its place among the lives—the trees, the annual plants, the animals and birds, the living of all these and the dead—that go and have gone to make the life of the earth. I am less important than I thought. . . . My mind loses its urgings, senses its nature, and is free."

Reading such passages, I'm inspired to get out of my house, walk around the block, and breathe some fresh air. I also yearn for extended days and nights in the natural world, which I know to be one of the most reliable balms for my soul. As I settled into the fourth week of my wilderness sojourn, I was exhilarated by the rare gift of experiencing nature in a raw, undisturbed form. On some days, I was awestruck by the beauty of a landscape that barely had been touched by human activity:

FEBRUARY 11—DAY 24

This morning I scrambled up a steep slope to the top of the ridge that separates the ranch from its southern drainage. Fantastic view in all directions, and no sign of humans anywhere. There must be 200 square miles in view and not so much as a road grade, telephone pole, or fence line disturbs them. I felt a great stirring in my heart, a pulsing emotion that seemed equal parts excitement, sadness, and foreboding. It was so poignant that all I could do was stand and take it all in, the usual train of words in my head screeching to an abrupt halt. When they started up again, I realized what this storm of feeling was about. I was excited to be in the midst of such human-free, pristine wilderness; deeply sad that such an infinitesimal percentage of the world's people would ever witness such a breath-catching scene; and struck by a foreboding that all this was vanishing from every corner of the Earth where it remained, except for Antarctica, faster than anyone could do very much about.

The transformative power of nature takes many forms. As a source of your own inspiration, I urge you to use a personal journal to record your own thoughts and feelings about quiet alone-time in nature, along with any other insights or understandings that come to you through your personal exploration of silence and solitude. Keep in mind, however, that acquiring new perspectives and making observations are not necessarily among the goals of fully inhabiting such stillness. Rather, they may just as easily derive from the full awareness of an open heart and an observing mind. Both are available to us if we cultivate the mindful presence that is often a gift of quiet alone-time.

CHAPTER TEN

GROWING FROM THE STILLNESS

The place of being still and connecting to
something deeper within ourselves is available
at every moment. I've discovered that the more
stressful and chaotic things are on the outside,
the calmer I have to get on the inside.

—Oprah Winfrey, O magazine, July 2001

One of the most challenging aspects of taking extended time to embrace silence and solitude is coming back to mundane daily routines. Some difficulty is expected, such as readjustment to the pervasive noise and fast pace of modern life. Other tasks are more surprising: how to respond to those who ask about quiet alone-time with genuine interest as well as those who seem oblivious or even hostile to our experience. Finally, there are the completely unexpected and cascading reactions that do not surface until days or weeks have passed.

Exploration of our inner world through silence and solitude may stir deep emotions that do not necessarily well to the surface until an unknown cue draws them out. This is the fruit we grow in stillness that may nourish (or deplete) us in ways that cannot be savored fully during the initial experience.

I was struck head-on by this reality a few weeks after ending my long retreat in the wilderness. Still emotionally porous and vulnerable, I broke down in tears while driving past a florist's display of Mother's Day roses. "Remember Mom on Her Day," the sign in the shop commanded. At that time, my mother was in the middle stages of the Alzheimer's disease that would eventually kill her. The tender feelings triggered by this reminder of Mom's love coincided at that moment with a program I was listening to on the radio about the special needs of individuals confined to wheelchairs. Since one of my brothers was severely disabled—never able to walk—the topic was close to my heart. Those long weeks of quiet alone-time had given me immediate access to the well of emotions surrounding these two family members and I felt I had no choice but to pull the car over and cry. The hot tears of this cathartic moment cooled my inflamed heart.

At other times, when I might be more "in my head," I am sure I would not have felt such intense sadness. In this instance, however, expressing my grief felt healing and soothing. My subsequent experience has shown that quiet alone-time has the power to connect me to any emotion that is striving to be acknowledged. These feelings run the gamut from fear of failure to pleasure of friendship, from anger over mistreatment to delight in success. The pregnant stillness of silence and solitude may birth an urge to laugh or a desire to be sexual, a dread of dealing with a difficult colleague or a sense of awe concerning the mysteries of life. While many of these latent emotions may come as a surprise, I prefer to think of them as a kind of letter from God, delivered from the unconscious and waiting for us to discover what message they bring.

NOTING WHAT ARISES DURING YOUR QUIET ALONE-TIME

Within the graceful spaciousness of silence and solitude, thoughts and emotions may emerge that are obscured from our consciousness by the tumult and diversion of daily life. While not all of what arises is pleasant or soothing, what's most important is that it arises at all. Feelings and beliefs that are uncomfortable or confusing deserve to be examined and dealt with. Honor them by writing them down or talking about them with a confidante so that you can reflect on their significance and learn more about what such insights mean.

There are many paths on the journey to greater self-awareness and openness. Following one route that leads to silence and solitude does not preclude others. Yet no matter what route you take, a common destination remains: the ability to cultivate a sense of wholeness and unity. The human desire to feel more fully integrated, aware, and satisfied with what life has to offer is universal.

Tuning in to the present moment is only the beginning of a transformative process that, if we choose to pursue it, has no end. Time spent mindfully in silence and solitude can dissolve many of the familiar boundaries we feel between "self" and "other," between "the world inside" and "the world outside," between "the observer" and "the observed." The implications are profound, for it is difficult to awaken to the truths that lie within ourselves without also discovering fundamental truths that lie beyond us.

Quiet alone-time isn't a prerequisite for happiness or contentment, but our values and priorities may shift when we encounter ourselves in silence and solitude. You might find your "needs" may change after you come to stillness and contemplate your place in the universe.

British philosopher E. F. Schumacher probed the implications of this expanded consciousness in his book, *A Guide for the Perplexed*. "It is a grave error to accuse a man who pursues self-knowledge of 'turning his back on society,'" Schumacher wrote. "The opposite would be more

EAST MEETS WEST

"It is our basic right to be a happy person," believes the Dalai Lama. "That should be our goal." Speaking in 2001 at the University of Wisconsin's Keck Laboratory for Functional Brain Imaging and Behavior, Tibet's revered spiritual leader was quick to add that "scientists, no matter how great, cannot prove Nirvana. That is our business."

The Dalai Lama's visit to the university coincided with a two-day conference focusing on whether sitting in meditation can transform the brain in beneficial ways. Researchers at the Madison campus are tracing the chemical roots of emotions in the brain and using noninvasive methods to scan the brains of Buddhists as they meditate. According to Keck director Richard Davidson in the summer 2001 issue of *On Wisconsin,* many scientists now are convinced that meditation brings about changes in brain chemistry that lead to better health and well-being. Davidson told the Dalai Lama about ways in which an exploration of silence and solitude, in the form of nonreligious meditation, might be very useful as a therapy for treatment of chronic pain and other ailments. The Dalai Lama replied, "That's wonderful!"

---

nearly true: that a man who fails to pursue self-knowledge is and remains a danger to society, for he will tend to misunderstand everything that other people say or do, and remain blissfully unaware of the significance of many of the things he does himself."

Centuries earlier, the Greek philosopher Aristotle admonished his disciples: "Know thyself." This declaration is as powerful as it is simple. The person who eschews self-knowledge may stumble through life as a sleepwalker, never drinking from the "spring overflowing its springbox," as the Sufi poet Jelaluddin Rumi called the fount of wisdom that flows deeply within each of us, waiting to be discovered. The implications of looking inward are fathomless, yet the choice to do so is always ours alone to make. In a modern world where we are easily seduced by delusion and distraction, this is not easy.

Ancient Chinese sages believed that when a student was ready, the right teacher would appear. When a person was motivated and receptive, the appropriate wisdom—sometimes conveyed through experience rather than by a human teacher—presented itself. Philosophers from other cultures, along with contemporary experts on child development, echo similar convictions that we learn best when conditions are ripe, facilitated by our strong desire to acquire a specific type of knowledge.

Silence and solitude are two such teachers. They are as accessible as the next moment, as transformative as light, and as powerful as they are common. The wisdom they can bring us has life-changing potential. The paradox is that finding the hushed, serene places where these teachers dwell is at once deceptively easy and maddeningly hard, particularly in the world at present. The potential rewards, however, are well worth the formidable undertaking.

An embrace of silence and solitude allows us to touch the fullness of possibility, awakening to the cause and effect of our lives. Quiet alone-time opens up space for observations, musings, and reflections. Being a healthy human, engaged in life and accepting ourselves in a loving way, demands self-awareness. If a person never stops to listen to his or her heart and mind, how can he or she begin to know—much less under-stand—what is truly felt, valued, thought, known, and wanted?

FINDING YOUR WAY TO THE STRESS-FREE ZONE

Elaine St. James, author of the best-selling book Simplify Your Life *and a newspaper column of the same name, offers a few tips from her own life about how to maintain access to silence and solitude while moving into what she calls, "the stress-free zone." Here is a sampling, summarized from St. James's writings:*

• *Get up earlier. This mandate might mean rising at 5 A.M. (after going to bed at about 10 P.M. the night before) in order to have an unhurried morning routine. For St. James, the latter often includes meditating, taking a walk with her husband, reading, thinking, and enjoying a leisurely breakfast. Sometimes she uses the earliest hours of the day to "do nothing" or, if she feels the need, to stay in bed a while longer and enjoy some extra sleep.*

• *Schedule regular intervals in which one can be silent and alone. St. James established this by excusing herself from the company of others during lunch time each Friday. She later extended the withdrawal by several hours until it filled almost all of Friday. St. James uses her weekly quiet alone-time to, among other things, think about her life and what she wants it to be. She regards the silence of these hours as sacred and does not allow anyone—including friends and members of her family—to break this routine, although she will occasionally do so herself if a critical deadline must be met.*

- *Schedule solo getaways. It may be a weekend or a full week, but extended time away from others allows St. James to build some space around her work, family, and social obligations. Sometimes her sojourns involve leaving town, while others are created at home by disconnecting and ignoring (or letting someone else handle) all avenues of incoming communications. This means turning off telephones, ignoring e-mail, not answering the doorbell, and so on. St. James finds that keeping the rest of life's routines simple makes it easier for her to arrange such departures now than in the past.*

Since silence and solitude are our teachers, we need to work to protect them. Although the world is ever noisier and more frenetic, a backlash is building. If successful, direct action may help preserve some islands of silence, solitude, and stillness, while reducing the overall din of modern life. I encourage you to learn about noise pollution ordinances in your community—if they don't exist, lobby for them—and see that they are enforced aggressively.

The nascent antinoise movement has much in common with campaigns that nonsmokers and their organizations have waged over the years for restrictions on public smoking, and the battles that members of Mothers Against Drunk Driving have fought to keep alcohol drinkers from endangering others on public roads. The bottom line for all these activists is managing aspects of modern life that are demonstrably dangerous. Because the potential negative health effects of excessive noise are well documented, it is this aspect of the problem that is receiving the most attention and may be the most powerful lever for change in human behavior and public policy.

"It used to be cool to smoke and no one would ask you to put out a cigarette," recalled Nancy Nadler, director of the Noise Center of the nonprofit League for the Hard of Hearing, in a 2000 interview with Kathryn Rem for the *Springfield State Journal*. All that changed with the widespread understanding that secondhand smoke can promote deadly diseases or chronic ailments. Nadler went on to predict that, in the same way that most of America's public buildings are now smoke-free, some day we will have "quiet zones" established in offices and shopping districts. These have already existed for years around hospitals.

Nadler believes that sanctuaries of silence will become more common as compelling links are drawn between excessive noise and such potentially stress-related health problems as depression, heart disease, anxiety, and insomnia. "A life intruded upon by repeated noise is certainly not a life of pleasure and contentment," Nadler pointed out. "The more people ask for [peace and quiet], the more acceptable it will become."

Gordon Hempton, the recorder of natural sounds mentioned in chapter four, now lobbies for the preservation of silence in pristine natural environments. He believes we need such places in order to calm and revitalize our turbulent souls, while reminding ourselves of the primal rhythms of a world beyond human influence. The gradual increase in the background noise of modern life, Hempton pointed out in a 2000 *Audubon* magazine interview, has even forced us to talk louder. In 1990, he notes, the volume level of an animated conversation was typically around fifty-five decibels. As this book was written, in 2002, the average reported volume was sixty-five decibels, or a 20 percent increase within a dozen years. The experience of Bernie Krause, another nature recordist, also confirms this trend. Krause reports that whereas it once took him ten to fifteen hours to record one hour of useful material untainted by human noise; it now takes two thousand.

TAKE A DAY OFF

Even the most relaxed and mindful person can feel stressed by the demands of everyday life: work deadlines, family pressures, personal commitments, and unexpected crises that seem to arise inevitably at the worst possible times. One solution is to excuse yourself from as many responsibilities as possible for twenty-four hours. Call it a "mental health" day or a "time out." Make sure you don't waste this mini-break, however. Advance planning will help you get the most out of your brief escape from the pressures of modern life. Some suggestions:

- *Seek and enjoy silence and solitude. Spend time in nature, sit in meditation, take a walk, or indulge in a sauna or hot tub soak. Resist the telephone, computer, and TV.*

- *Give time to what you love most: family, spouse, a hobby, exercise, or anything that gives you pleasure and feels neglected.*

- *Do one thing at a time, and give it your undivided attention. Multitasking makes it hard to enjoy any of the several activities you are juggling. It also tends to drain energy and increase stress.*

- *Avoid some decisions. Let others decide what to eat, where to go, and how to interact. This is particularly important for those of us who ordinarily make lots of decisions.*

- *Avoid clocks and do something that's so absorbing that you lose track of time.*

- *If you can't sit still, get rid of clutter. Extra and unwanted things take up space and absorb our energy because they take time to organize and maintain. You'll feel lighter if you get rid of only ten things you know you are unlikely to ever use again.*

- *Make a list of what's most important to you, then reflect on how many of these things you are actually getting at present. If you want more of life's rewards, zero in on ways to get them.*

Cellular telephones, while convenient, are often singled out as a potential nuisance by those in search of public peace and quiet. It's not merely the noise stemming from their public use that's bothersome, but the implied assumption that the user must always be available. "The phone can ring, quite literally, anywhere on the planet," essayist and short story writer Mark Slouka noted in a 1999 *Harper's Magazine* essay. "This is not necessarily good news."

Statistics confirm the obvious: the time Americans spend on the telephone increased 24 percent during the first seven years that cellular telephones were available. Being "out" is no longer an employee option, since technology helps one to be always "in." The result is that some people now take it as a personal insult when others cannot be reached by telephone. A survey of executives concluded that many have doubled their workload since getting such gadgets. "But I don't want to be available all the time," one New York businessman told me during a 2001 visit to Manhattan. "Sometimes I just want to be left alone." Those of us who feel our right to silence is usurped by ringing cell phones and those who converse on them in public may some day have laws to protect us.

Henry David Thoreau, who found it difficult to bear the human-made noises and intrusions of the comparatively serene 1840s, would be appalled by the sounds saturating the urban landscape of the twenty-first century. "I love a wide margin to my life," Thoreau wrote during his famous retreat at Walden Pond. Yet even at the time of the writer's residence, Walden was only somewhat rural, its peacefulness punctuated several times each day by the roar and whistle of trains passing along one edge of the pond.

SYMPTOMS OF A HURRY-UP WORLD

People are moving around the clock, every day of the week. No wonder a short-hand term—24/7—has been coined to describe nonstop activity or availability. One does not have to look far to see evidence of the ways our society is influenced by the frenetic pace to which we have fallen prey:

- In *Time for Life,* John P. Robinson and Geoffrey Godbey describe recent police department studies showing that drivers exceed the posted speed limit, on average, by ten miles an hour.

- Executives and office workers are asking manufacturers to make elevator doors close faster. The average speed of closure, according to Otis Elevator Company, is already four seconds. Obviously, this is not fast enough for some time-conscious employees.

- Single-serving packaging has become enormously popular, although one *New York Times* test reported in the *Santa Fe New Mexican* on April 9, 2000 found that one such breakfast item cut preparation time by only one second (down to thirteen seconds from fourteen).

- Accoring to industry estimates in a report published in the *New York Times* on October 23, 2001, sales of audio books are up, apparently because many people have no time to read the print versions and they spend more time commuting and taking business trips than ever before.

- The December 10, 1994 edition of the *Hartford Courant* reported that the average length of TV news stories has shrunk to well below sixty seconds; sound bites used within such stories are often fifteen seconds or less.

- According to an article by Richard Ford in the December 27, 1998 edition of the *New York Times,* information phone operators now use computers that edit out the "ums" and "ahs" when callers speak, so their hesitations will not waste the operators' time.

- Place-based media—distribution of advertising in places where people work, study, play, travel, and wait—has expanded to include airports, stores, doctors' offices, classrooms, health clubs, subway platforms, hospitals, post offices, theme parks, theaters, and fast-food restaurants.

"My nearest neighbor is a mile distant," Thoreau wrote of Walden. "[Yet] I have never felt lonesome, nor oppressed by a sense of solitude."

What Thoreau craved, as expressed in his old-fashioned prose, was sufficient quiet alone-time to contemplate, to think, to feel, and simply to "be." In other writings, Thoreau described a preference for his own interior dialogue over the superficial conversations that he often encountered when socializing. "I feel it wholesome to be alone the greater part of the time," Thoreau confessed. "To be in company, even with the best, is soon wearisome and dissipating. I love to be alone. I never found the companion who was so companionable as solitude."

More than a century and a half later, another American writer expressed a similar sentiment about the shallow content found in the sea of words that now washes over us each day. In his *Harper's* essay, Mark Slouka contended that even though we are presently "locked in a grid of sound, lashed by infinite channels, we are alone in our babel, impoverished by our communications." Our expanded capacity to communicate does not necessarily ensure that we have anything important to say to each other.

Are people like Slouka and Thoreau misanthropes, who would just as soon live on a planet as empty of humans as possible? This is one plausible interpretation of their screeds against noise and crowds. Yet there is ample evidence to support their invective. In the twenty-first century we are forced to adjust to the ubiquitous noise of commerce and communication as silence is pushed to the edges of daily life: the wee hours of the morning, for example, and places where nobody lives. We deny the fact that our information surplus and activity overload entraps and fragments us, further alienating us from authentic, nature-made sounds and unadorned, luxurious silence. The rising tide of people-created sound signals a society that is moving too fast and too loudly for its own good. Our ability to adapt to the speed of the Information Age is being tested, perhaps exceeded.

The flood of messages that wash over us, like the downpours of midsummer thunderstorms, give us too much too quickly. We glean little that lasts, and risk being unable to discriminate that which is truly valuable. The data deluge represents information moving much too fast to become knowledge and slowly develop into wisdom. As such, it neither recharges nor illuminates, tending instead to increase confusion and befuddlement, while leaving us feeling paralyzed and overwhelmed. Our responses become less informed and less thoughtful. Geared toward impulsive, rote reactions and instant, self-absorbed gratification, we seem less able to foresee what is headed our way and more ignorant of what it takes to sustain our lives in a healthy manner. One apparent victim is our willingness and ability to make carefully reasoned decisions and execute long-term planning.

In part as a result of the tyranny of speed and society's purposeful dismissal of silence, many of us feel psychic isolation, chronic impatience, and emotional poverty within the clouds of unwanted diversion and unbidden noise that surrounds us. But even this hunger and discomfort is exploited: money buys space, and space buys silence.

Take a look at any upscale travel magazine or Website and you will find luxury resorts and exclusive spas advertising getaways that can protect guests from the vagaries of the outside world, including its hullabaloo and strife. The trend around the world, in developing nations as well as those that are highly industrialized, is to buy and sell the "choice" of experiencing quiet alone-time to the highest bidder. The more silence and solitude available in a given place, the higher the price paid to obtain it. Part of what a guest pays for at an expensive hotel, for example, is the privilege of not having to listen to the public din of noisy neighbors and clanking factories that individuals of lesser means (or customers of cheaper hotels) must put up with every day. In a similar mode, the gated communities of the wealthy manage to avoid the jarring fragmentation and tightly interwoven domains of low-rent folks.

Even in wilderness areas, those of us who have the means are reaching for our wallets to be whisked by horseback, snowmobile, or helicopter to remote locations where only the occasional airplane intrudes. Want to really get away from it all? For a price, you can be taken as far as you like, including Antarctica and the North Pole.

The future will be only more crowded. The nonprofit group, Population Connection, reported that experts predict more than 30 megacities, with populations of more than 25 million, will emerge by 2020. Their residents will live in the human equivalent of beehives and anthills, surviving on a media diet delivered on TV, computer, and movie screens. For these millions, there will be no silent dawns, trickling brooks, or pine-scented forests. They may become indifferent to the concept of quiet alone-time, having never known it. The experience of silence and solitude among this growing majority may become extinct without the slightest ripple of regret, so alien as to be undiscovered and therefore unwanted.

THE SILENCE OF THE TALK SHOW HOST

In early 2001, TV talk-show maven Oprah Winfrey asked renowned Buddhist meditation teacher Sharon Salzberg to lead a weekend silent meditation retreat at Winfrey's bucolic Indiana farm. Along with Salzberg and her host, retreat participants included several of Winfrey's friends and a yoga instructor. Although she is a long-time "morning meditator," Winfrey reported in her magazine, *Oprah,* that maintaining silence for the two-day period was a bigger challenge than she had expected. However, her concluding thoughts were positive.

"[Silent meditation] showed me that one reason I can stay sane and feel balanced and connected is because I practice being mindful and getting quiet in structured and unstructured ways," wrote Winfrey. "I try to stay conscious of every moment. . . . By going silent, I can bring more energy to [my] voice when I do speak. . . . Our real power comes from knowing who we are and what we're here to do— and that begins with looking inside ourselves in silence. Solitude is part of the path to spiritual awareness."

Thankfully, despite the gradual disappearance of silence and solitude from public places, many options remain for those seeking quiet alone-time. Hundreds of secluded retreat centers, for example, offer sanctuaries where one can become immersed in silence and solitude for as little as a few hours or as long as several years. Social commentator Pico Iyer, who has reported about the transformative power of travel and meditation, joins monastic communities (often Christian or Buddhist) to guarantee himself the solitude he depends on to create new literary work. Without these time-outs, Iyer says he feels too distracted, too pulled by interruptions, to get much high-quality writing done. The result is a kind of alienation from direct experience that is made illusory by the ease of modern travel and the ubiquity of communications gadgets.

"We may find that we have more and more 'connections' in the telephone, or airplane, senses, and fewer and fewer in the classic human sense," wrote Iyer in his book, *The Global Soul.* As someone of Indian ancestry who was born in England and raised in California, Iyer is a living example of how the meaning of borders and identities has shifted. Our boundaries today are not so much *physical,* he suggests, as they are *experiential.* We have many ways of communicating electronically, but seem increasingly disconnected from the most basic experiences of being alive, including the direct experience of silence and solitude.

"A republic founded on 'the pursuit of happiness' seems a culture destined for disappointment," Iyer writes, "if only because it's pursuing something that, by definition, doesn't come from being sought."

In researching this book, I met a man who so enjoyed the peacefulness of a silence-shrouded monastery in a remote New Mexico that he became a permanent resident, even though Fred is neither a monk nor Catholic. Fred works at the monastery's small gift shop, where he gets all the social contact he says he needs from the handful of visitors who stop in each day to buy carvings and other religious articles made by resident monks. "I am not evading people by living here," he told me. "I am simply choosing how much socializing I want to do. If that happens to be less than most people then, well, that's my choice. This life makes me very happy."

Such stories can be found almost everywhere. In rural Oregon, I met a sixty-one-year-old woman who told me about her past life as a supercharged public relations executive in downtown Chicago. "There were weeks in a row," she recalled, "when I would work around the clock, rush home, bathe, change my clothes, nuke a meal, wolf it down, and go straight back to my office." Now this lively divorcee lives on her savings, investments, and Social Security. The Midwest transplant spends most days reading novels, puttering in her gardening, taking leisurely walks, and hobnobbing with friends. Her daughter and grandchildren visit regularly.

"During my first weeks here," the woman admitted, "I almost went nuts. I'd come here for peace and quiet and then I didn't have enough to do and I had all these habits I couldn't break, like reading four newspapers a day." A decade after her exit from the urban fast lane, she talked enthusiastically about her good fortune in having silence and solitude whenever she wants them, and the fellowship of good friends and interesting neighbors when she doesn't. "At last I've found perfect symmetry in my life," she concluded. "I've never felt healthier or happier."

A more extreme example of contentment with quiet alone-time is Everett Reuss, a young artist whose desire for wilderness beauty compelled him to wander alone (save the company of two burros) for months on end in the mountains and deserts of California and the Southwest. W. L. Rusho describes Reuss's story in *Everett Reuss: A Vagabond for Beauty.*

In 1934, at the age of twenty, Reuss disappeared in the rugged canyons of southern Utah and was never seen again. "This trip will be longer than I expected," Reuss wrote in a final letter to his brother, Waldo. "I will be in many beautiful places and I do not wish to taste, but to drink deep." His story has inspired a generation of vagabonds to set out in search of silence, solitude, and, so it seems, their souls.

"I have not tired of the wilderness," Everett told Waldo. "I prefer the saddle to the streetcar and the star-sprinkled sky to a roof; the obscure and difficult trail, leading into the unknown, to any paved highway; and the deep peace of the wild to the discontent bred by cities."

Although they have become more scarce and precious, pools of profound silence can still be found along the rugged trails that Reuss followed, breaking on the ear, as a more recent visitor put it, "like the tide of a great ocean." Such clear, clean eddies of solitude still possess a mysterious and miraculous ability to simultaneously calm and rejuvenate the human soul. Here we find an inward passage to moods, truths, memories, and states of mind that we might otherwise have no cause to explore. In quiet alone-time we often discover that which is only dimly known or deliberately ignored.

"We need sometimes," philosopher George Santayana wrote in *Soliloquies in England,* "to escape into open solitudes, into timelessness . . . in order to sharpen the edge of life, to taste hardship, and to be compelled to work desperately for a moment at no matter what." There is wisdom, Santayana concluded, "in turning as often as possible from the familiar to the unfamiliar." In silence and solitude we may feel a pull toward a place that is deep within ourselves, because it is in this rare space that we are drawn closer to who we really are—and aspire to become.

Finally, after more than three companionless months, my time of reflection in the alpine valley came to an end. Drifts of snow were still higher than my head in places, but the owner of the ranch was able, with great difficulty, to drive in and pick me up. Our first stop on the "outside" was a nondescript gas station and convenience store in a small village at the base of the mountains.

"Pick out something you'd like to eat," the rancher insisted. "I'll pay for it."

I looked around at the hundreds of food items that were available to me, even though the one-room grocery was tiny.

"I can't decide," I stammered, feeling frozen in my tracks. "It's too overwhelming."

For the next several weeks, those were the words I would use to describe my experience of almost everything that happened to me. Even sitting in a popular restaurant, surrounded by bustling waiters and chattering customers, with music playing in the background, was almost too much to take in. This process of readjustment was a dramatic reminder of how much we deal with in the course of a typical day. No wonder we often feel stressed, and in need of quiet alone-time on a regular basis:

APRIL 25—4 DAYS AFTER MY RETURN

Reintegrating with the fast-paced and crazy-making world is more difficult than I anticipated. My mood swings are extreme and I feel a tenuous grip on my sanity much of the time. It's hard to sleep and even harder to be awake.

APRIL 26—5 DAYS AFTER MY RETURN

I woke up early this morning, feeling like a raw wound.

MAY 15—24 DAYS AFTER MY RETURN

My transition remains difficult and by now I think I will never be the same. I can't get used to many of the differences between this reality and the one I experienced at the ranch, but I don't think I am meant to. I am meant to stay in touch with the lessons I learned.

I am riding a roller coaster of emotions, sometimes falling into inexplicable tears and sometimes soaring with happiness. And, of course, all sorts of feelings in between. My heart feels open, but not quite as tender as it did at first. Yet I will survive. I always do.

I am trying to revive old friendships and make new ones. I've never appreciated the value of friends as much as I do now. And I've never regretted more my carelessness in the way I've treated them. I will never do that again. The changes have gone into effect and I'm already feeling the results. There are many people who care about me, thank God. I am trying to focus on the positive. Some days it's easy, some days it's hard. I am confronting the whole range of emotions, which I am at last learning to integrate. I'm glad I'm here, back in my home.

The wilderness retreat has changed my perspective on everything. I am mindful of the actions I take. I want a new kind of vision, at all levels. I know I need more balance in my life. I also know that, from here, I can't go back.

As I complete this book, it is four years since my return from the wilderness. I go back to the ranch at least once each summer, spending a week there in relative silence and solitude. I sleep under the stars; camp in the meadow; meditate in the cabin; and hike among the streams, crags, and forests. The coyotes and beavers seem like old friends. And so does the quiet alone-time.

Not all the "positive" changes I underwent took hold. Some of my "negative" habits and routines have crept back, to my dismay. But to a considerable extent, the personal growth I experienced influences me almost constantly in what I feel and think, how I act and respond, and the way I manage my life. I don't fulfill my own intention of embracing silence and solitude every single day, but I still come close. The rewards of quiet alone-time have been greater than I could ever describe to you and most of these benefits are beyond the capacity of mere words. Now it is time for you to discover them on your own.

In this book I purposely have not provided a detailed road map for personal transformation through the exploration of silence and solitude. I offer no specific prescription regarding the "best" application of quiet alone-time, other than to emphasize that self-discipline and commitment are powerful allies that take us to deeper levels of experience, knowledge, and power. Ultimately, the potential gifts of silence, solitude, and stillness are unique to you. The wisest integration of their teachings is subjective, and no one else can know the most effective way to employ them. What's more, your need for quiet alone-time may wax and wane over time, depending on the circumstances of your life and your own temperament.

While the embrace of silence, solitude, and stillness is highly individualistic, it reveals and strengthens our commonalty as humans. By taking time to stop and peer inward with an attitude of openness and acceptance, we encounter the same spectrum of strengths and weaknesses, joys and sorrows, frustrations and contentments that we witness in others each day. From this calm yet awakened state of clear seeing emerges the potential for personal growth and transformation.

When I emerged from ninety-seven days alone in the wilderness, I felt that in many respects I had become a different person. Not all of those "differences" took root, though, and some shifts in my behavior, attitude, and thinking that I expected to last, did not. Others have remained without apparent effort on my part. The vast majority of changes that I have sought to preserve, however, have been retained, modified, and bolstered through my (almost) daily ritual of embracing quiet alone-time.

"Silence," wrote Herman Melville in his novel, *Pierre, or, the Ambiguities,* "is the only voice of our God." Melville left few clues as to what he meant by this provocative statement. I interpret him to mean that we must cease making our own noise if we hope to receive fully the quiet wisdom of nature and the deep truths within our hearts. If we continue to surround ourselves with distracting noise and push ourselves through constant movement, we will inevitably keep craving their opposite. This hunger is for a silent sanctuary that affords us the priceless gift of looking at our lives in the relief of stillness, knowing that simplicity is real wealth and solitude is good company. It is as accessible as the next moment, as simple as being alone.

RECOMMENDED SOURCES FOR EXPLORING SILENCE AND SOLITUDE

RECOMMENDED READING

General

Abbey, Edward. *Down the River.* New York: Plume/Pantheon, 1991.

Anderson, Joan. *A Year by the Sea: Thoughts of an Unfinished Woman.* New York: BantamDoubledayDell, 2000.

Baetz, Ruth. *Wild Communion: Experiencing Peace in Nature.* Center City, MN: Hazelden, 1997.

A Seattle-area psychotherapist provides an inspiring and practical guide for making regular connections with nature part of everyday life, with the goal of enhanced serenity and a greater sense of well-being. There are meditations and action steps in each chapter, with emphasis on how the urban resident can easily experience nature.

Beston, Henry. *The Outermost House: A Year of Life on the Great Beach of Cape Cod.* New York: Henry Holt, 1992.

Buchholz, Ester Schaler. *The Call of Solitude: Alonetime in a World of Attachment.* New York: Simon & Schuster, 1997.

A psychologist's look at ways to cultivate a positive appreciation of solitude.

Budbill, David. *Moment to Moment.* New York: Consortium, 1999.

Chah, Achaan. *A Still Forest Pool.* Wheaton, IL: (Quest Books) Theosophical Publishing House, 1985.

Davis, Bruce. *Monastery Without Walls: Daily Life in the Silence.* Berkeley: Celestial Arts, 1995.

Out of print but available at www.Universe.com. The author believes a sacred inner life takes root in solitude and time committed to development of a spiritual practice. Davis describes a wide range of pathways to spirituality and an ongoing personal celebration of the sacred, along with a discussion of some of the obstacles to such explorations, including fear, loneliness, and self-importance.

Dominguez, Joe and Vicki Robin. *Your Money or Your Life: Transforming Your*

Relationship with Money and Achieving Financial Independence. New York: Penguin Books, 1992, 1999.

Douglas, David. *Wilderness Sojourn: Notes on the Desert Silence.* New York: HarperCollins, 1989.

Dowrick, Stephanie. *Intimacy and Solitude.* New York: W.W. Norton and Co., 1996.

Cofounder of Women's Press and a practicing psychotherapist in England, Dowrick discusses the interdependent nature of intimacy and solitude. She argues that childhood experiences with solitude can affect adult intimacy, maintaining that the less one needs others, the more easily he or she can embrace them. The author draws on her own experiences, those of her patients, and theories put forward by various psychologists.

France, Peter. *Hermits: The Insights of Solitude.* New York: St. Martin's Press, 1996.

The author, who spends much of his time living in an eremitic manner on a Greek island, explores the history of hermits—including naturalist Henry David Thoreau and Hindu mystic Ramakrishna—and shares some of the truths they found in solitude. France describes the hermit life as an antidote to disillusionment with the world of humanity and as a guide to rediscovering our true selves. He explores the Western tradition and justification of living alone, dating back to the era of Socrates in ancient Greece.

Fromm, Pete. *Indian Creek Chronicles: A Winter Alone in the Wilderness.* New York: St. Martin's, 1993.

A young man spends seven months virtually alone in a wilderness tent in Idaho, spinning a good-humored tale of self-sufficiency and personal transformation in the process. His experience of isolation and risk are contrasted with the easy affluence of life in modern America.

Glassman, Bernie and Rick Fields. *Instructions to the Cook: A Zen Master's Lessons in Living a Life that Matters.* New York: Bell Tower, 1996.

Gleick, James. *Faster.* New York: Vintage Books, 2000

Goethe, Johann Wolfgang von. *Criticisms, Reflections, and Maxims of Goethe.* Philadelphia: Richard West, 1989.

Halifax, Joan. *The Fruitful Darkness: Reconnecting in the Body of the Earth.* New York: HarperCollins, 1993.

Hanh, Thich Nhat. *The Heart of Understanding.* Berkeley: Parallax Press, 1988.
———. *Teaching Peace.* Berkeley: Parallax Press, 1992.

Holland, Barbara. *One's Company.* North Pomfret, VT: Trafalgar Square, 2000.

Iyer, Pico. *The Global Soul: Jet Lag, Shopping Malls, and the Search for Home.* New York: Knopf, 2000.

Jarvis, Cheryl. *The Marriage Sabbatical: The Journey That Brings You Home.*
New York: Broadway Books, 2002.
The author describes her experience of leaving her husband and
children for three months in order to live and work alone. Jarvis goes
on to tell the stories of fifty-five other married women in mid-life who
experienced "sabbaticals" from their families. Their various accounts
support the notion that such intervals can help a woman gain
confidence, restore energy, and develop important insights, often
revitalizing her relationships with her husband and children.

Kabat-Zinn, Jon. *Full Catastrophe Living: Using the Wisdom of Your Body and
Mind to Face Stress, Pain, and Illness.* New York: Delta, 1990.

————. *Wherever You Go, There You Are.* New York: Hyperion, 1999.

Katz, Jon. *Running to the Mountain: A Journey of Faith and Change.* New York:
Broadway Books, 1999.
At age fifty, journalist and suburban family man Jon Katz buys a
dilapidated cabin in upstate New York and confronts his long-held
questions about his mortality, self-worth, and spirituality. He comes
away with a renewed appreciation for all that is important to him. This
memoir focuses in particular on the writings of Trappist monk Thomas
Merton on the subject of solitude.

Kottler, Jeffrey A. *Private Moments, Secret Selves: Enriching Our Time Alone.*
New York: Ballantine, 1991.
A detailed summary of suggestions for making effective use of solitude.

Kroeber, Theodora. *Ishi in Two Worlds.* Berkeley: University of California
Press, 1981.

Kundtz, David. *Stopping: How to Be Still When You Have to Keep Going.*
Berkeley, CA: Conari Press, 1998.
Written by a psychotherapist and former priest, this book describes
"doing nothing, as much as possible, for a definite period of time" as a
technique for reducing everyday stress and redirecting one's life to a
more purposeful and serene focus.

Lindbergh, Anne Morrow. *Gift from the Sea.* New York: Pantheon, 1991.

Mahler, Richard and Connie Goldman. *Secrets of Becoming a Late Bloomer.*
Center City, MN: Hazelden, 1999.

————. *Tending the Earth; Mending the Spirit: The Healing Gifts of Gardening.*
Center City, MN: Hazelden, 1999.

Merton, Thomas. *Thoughts in Solitude.* New York: Farrar, Straus and Giroux,
1989.
A book of meditations by a Catholic monk and philosopher who spent
much of his life in monasteries. Includes thirty-five pages on writing
about "the love of solitude." Merton offers a decidedly Christian point
of view about the value of solitude as it relates to prayer and other
forms of communion with God as well as nature.

Mitchell, Stephen, trans. *The Tao Te Ching*. By Lao-Tzu. Boston: Shambhala, 1998.

Moran, Victoria. *A Shelter for the Spirit: How to Make Your Home a Haven in a Hectic World*. New York: HarperCollins, 1997.

Murray, John A., ed. *The Quotable Nature Lover*. New York: The Lyons Press, 1999.

Nisker, Wes. *Buddha's Nature: Evolution as a Practical Guide to Enlightenment*. New York: Bantam, 1998.

Norris, Kathleen. *Amazing Grace: A Vocabulary of Faith*. New York: Riverhead, 1999.

Rechtschaffen, Stephen. *Time Shifting: Creating More Time to Enjoy Your Life*. New York: Doubleday, 1997.

Rilke, Rainer Maria. *Letters to a Young Poet*. New York: W.W. Norton, 1994.

Robinson, John P. and Geoffrey Godbey. *Time for Life: The Surprising Ways Americans Use Their Time*. Pittsburgh: Penn State Press, 2000.

Rusho, W. L. *Everett Reuss: A Vagabond for Beauty*. Salt Lake City: Gibbs Smith, 1985.

Santorelli, Saki. *Heal Thy Self: Lessons on Mindfulness in Medicine*. New York: Bell Tower, 2000.

Sarton, May. *Journal of a Solitude*. New York: W.W. Norton, 1973.
The best-selling journal of the late poet, essayist, and novelist, in which she expounds upon her love of nature and solitude. An illuminating exploration of the creative person's need for a quiet, serene space to work and reflect, in this case rural New England.

Selby, John. *Solitude: The Art of Living with Yourself*. Sante Fe: Heartsfire Books, 1998.
Selby is a practicing psychotherapist who believes that people who have difficulty relating to others must first learn how to relate to themselves if they hope to have better intimate relationships. This is a pragmatic and practical guide to loving and enjoying oneself so that one can share more with others. It balances theory and action plans, practical tips, and "how-to." Selby emphasizes balance and harmony in terms of the solitary and social parts of ourselves, with a focus on the reflection and pleasure that can be a part of solitude.

St. James, Elaine. *Simplify Your Life: 100 Ways to Slow Down and Enjoy the Things That Really Matter*. New York: Hyperion, 1989.
St. James is also the author of *Simplify Your Work Life* (Hyperion, 1994) and *Inner Simplicity* (Hyperion, 1995 and on audiotape from BantamDoubleday Dell, 1998).

Storr, Anthony. *Solitude: A Return to the Self*. New York: Ballantine Books, 1989.
The author of several books on psychology and an Oxford lecturer on

psychiatry, Storr explores the creative/intellectual mind and its attraction to solitude. In contrast to the emphasis on well-being as measured in relationship to other, the book argues that true mental health and happiness is ultimately based upon the ability to live in peace with oneself. Storr profiles Beethoven, Goya, Kipling, and Wittgenstein, among others, as he probes the close tie between imagination and abstract thought and the need for solitude.

Tolle, Eckhart. *The Power of Now.* Novato, CA: New World Library, 1999.

Thoreau, Henry David. *Walden.* Boston: Houghton Mifflin, 1949.

VanderBroeck, Goldian, ed. *Less Is More: The Art of Voluntary Poverty, an Anthology of Ancient and Modern Voices Raised in Praise of Simplicity.* Rochester, VT: Inner Traditions International, 1991.

Williams, Terry Tempest. *An Unspoken Hunger.* New York: Vantage, 1995.

Specific Benefits of Silence and Solitude

Casarjian, Robin. *Houses of Healing: A Prisoner's Guide to Inner Power and Freedom.* Boston: Lionheart Foundation, 1995.

Ellis, George A. *Inside Folsom Prison: Transcendental Meditation and TM-SIDHI Program.* Palm Springs, ETC., 1979.

Kabat-Zinn, Jon and Saki Santorelli (editors), *Mindfulness-Based Stress Reduction Professional Training Resource Manual.* Worcester, MA: Center for Mindfulness in Medicine, Health Care, and Society at Univ. of Massachusetts Medical School, 1999.

Lozoff, Bo. *We're All Doing Time.* Durham, NC: Hanuman Foundation, 1985.

Ornish, Dean. *Dr. Dean Ornish's Program for Reversing Heart Disease.* New York: Ballantine, 1996.

———. *Stress, Diet, and Your Heart.* New York: Signet/Penguin, 1984.

MAGAZINES AND NEWSLETTERS

General

Enough! Published by The Center for a New American Dream. (See p. 162)

Hope. Bimonthly magazine. Box 160, Naskeag Rd., Brooklin, ME 04616. *www.hopemag.com.*

Mother Earth News. Bimonthly magazine. Box 56302, Boulder, CO 80322. *www.motherearth.com.*

Organic Style: The Art of Living in Balance. 33 E. Minor St.; Emmaus; PA 18098. *www.organicstyle.com.*
Bimonthly publication with articles about health, fashion, travel, food, spirituality, and accomplished individuals, all from an "organic" or "balanced" lifestyle orientation.

The Sun. 107 N. Robertson St., Chapel Hill, NC 25716.

Monthly magazine with articles, interviews, poetry, and photographs that promote alternative ways of experiencing the world.

Utne. 1624 Harmon Place, Minneapolis, MN 55403.
Bimonthly mix of gleanings from other publications and original writing on a wide range of topics.

Specific Articles on the Benefits of Silence and Solitude

Barnes, Flo. "Prayer, Medicine, and Spirituality." *Santa Fe New Mexican* (April 14, 2000).

Brody, Howard. "Mind Over Medicine." *Psychology Today* (July/Aug. 2000).

Connie MacDougall. "All the Right Moves." *Seattle Times* (December 11, 1998).

Corliss, Richard. "The Power of Yoga." *Time* (April 23, 2001).

Cowell, Alan. "Cairo's Constant Din Getting People Down." *New York Times* (March 25, 1990).

Flaste, Richard. "The Power of Concentration." *Good Health Magazine* (a supplement of the *New York Times*) (October 8, 1989).

Goleman, Daniel. "The Brain Manages Happiness and Sadness in Different Centers." *New York Times* (Mar. 28, 1995).

Gorman, Christine. "Stressed Out Kids." *Time* (December 25, 2000).

Gudmestad, Julie. "Breathing Room." *Yoga Journal* (March/April 2002).

Guttman, Monika. "Are You Losing Your Mind?" *USA Weekend* (May 16, 1997).

Hales, Dianne and Robert E. Hales. "The Brain's Power to Heal." *Parade* (November 21, 1999).

Hamilton, Denise. "Health in Unlikely Settings." *Los Angeles Times* (Sept. 11, 2000).

Khalsa, Dharma Singh. "Holistic Health Advisor" *Yoga Journal* (Sept/Oct. 2000).

Labi, Nadya. "Om a Little Teapot." *Time* (February 19, 2001).

Mitchell, Tedd. "Using Meditation to Beat Stress." *USA Weekend* (June 6, 1999).

Noonan, David and Karen Springen. "The Prostate Plan." *Newsweek* (April 22, 2002).

Smith, Dennis. "The Heroes." *Newsweek* (September 9, 2002).

Taylor, Michael H. "The Missing Link." *Yoga Journal* (May/June 2001).

Winfrey, Oprah. "Inward Bound." *O* magazine (July 2001).

ORGANIZATIONS

Center for a New American Dream. 6930 Carroll Ave.,Takoma Park, MD
    20912. (800) 683-7326.
New Road Map Foundation. Box 15981, Seattle,WA 98115.
    Representing and furthering the work championed by Vicki Robin
    and the late Joe Dominguez.
Seeds of Simplicity. *www.seedsofsimplicity.org*.
Simple Living. *www.simpleliving.net*.
The Garden. *www.thegarden.net*.
The Natural Step. 116 New Montgomery St., #800, San Francisco, CA
    94105. (415) 318-8170.

RESOURCES FOR YOGA

A plethora of books and video tapes are available that provide instruction
on yoga postures and practices. Many libraries, bookstores, and video stores
carry this material, or check appropriate shopping sites on the Internet.
Many options are available to those who would like to try (or continue to
practice) yoga on their vacations. These range from specifically yoga-
themed workshops in exotic locations to classes on cruise ships, at health-
oriented spas or resorts, and as adjuncts to meditation retreats or
conferences. Several national magazines are devoted to yoga and associated
topics. Besides feature articles, they contain advertising for yoga-related
products such as mats, clothes, blocks, and so on.

Ansari, Mark and Liz Lark. *Yoga for Beginners*. New York: Carroll and
    Brown, Ltd., 1998.
Feuerstein, Georg. *The Shambhala Guide to Yoga*. Boston: Shambhala, 1996.
    An easy-to-use summary of the historical, spiritual, and philosophical
    underpinnings of yoga.
Kent, Howard. *Yoga Made Easy*. London: Quarto. 2002.
Kripalu Yoga. *www.kripalu.org*.
Shivapremananda, Swai. *Yoga for Stress Relief*. New York: Random House,
    1997.
Sivananda Yoga. *www.sivananda.org*.
Sivananda Yoga Center. *The Sivananda Companion to Yoga*. New York:
    Fireside, 2000.
Yoga Journal. 2054 University Ave., Berkeley, CA 94704.
    www.yogajournal.com.

RESOURCES FOR MEDITATION

Mindfulness-based meditation is also called "insight" or Vipassana meditation. Check listings for Buddhism or meditation under "churches" or "spiritual organizations" in newspapers, magazines, or phone directories published in your area. For a national listing of meditation groups and retreat centers involved in Vipassana Buddhism, obtain a copy of *The Inquiring Mind,* a free quarterly newspaper devoted to news about Vipassana meditation in the United States, Mexico, and Canada (see p. 163).

Many yoga centers and retreats include meditation and meditation instruction as part of their offerings to practitioners.

Retreat Centers
Insight Meditation Society. 1230 Pleasant St., Barre, MA 01005.
   (978) 355-4378. *www.dharma.org/ims.htm.*
Naropa University. 2130 Arapahoe Ave., Boulder, CO 80302.
   (303) 444-0702. *www.naropa.edu.*
Plum Village (founded by Vietnamese Zen master Thich Nhat Hanh).
   www.plumvillage.org.
Shambhala Mountain Center. 4921 County Road 68C, Red Feather Lakes,
   CO 80545. (970) 881-2184. *www.shambhalamountain.org.*
Spirit Rock Meditation Center. 5000 Sir Francis Drake Blvd., Woodacre,
   CA 94973. (415) 488-0164. *www.spiritrock.org.*
Upaya Zen Center. 1404 Cerro Grande Rd., Santa Fe, NM 87501.
   www.upaya.org.

Magazines
Buddhadharma: The Practitioner's Quarterly (published by *Shambhala Sun*), 1585
   Barrington St. #300, Halifax, NS, B3J 1Z8, Canada;
   www.buddhadharma.com
Parabola Magazine. 656 Broadway, New York, NY 10012. *www.parabola.org.*
   Quarterly.
Shambhala Sun: A Buddhist-Inspired Magazine, same address as above;
   (877) 786-1950; *www.shambhalasun.com.*
The Inquiring Mind. P.O. Box 9999, Berkeley, CA 94709. Biannual.
Tricycle: The Buddhist Review. 92 Vandam St., New York, NY 10013.
   www.tricycle.com. Quarterly.
Yoga Journal, 2054 University Ave., Berkeley, CA 94704; (510) 841-9200;
   www.yogajournal.com.

Books and Tapes

A catalog of audio tapes and CDs on Buddhism, yoga, personal transformation, and other topics is available from: Sounds True, 735 Walnut St., Boulder, CO 80302; (800) 333-9185.

Das, Lama Sarya. *Awakening the Buddha Within.* New York: Broadway
    Books, 1997.
Chodron, Pema. *When Things Fall Apart: Hearts Advice for Difficult Times.*
    Boston: Shambhala, 1997.
Dharma Seed Tape Library, Box 66, Wendel, Depot MA 01380.
    (800) 969-SEED. *www.dharmaseed.org.*
Goldstein, Joseph. *The Experience of Insight.* Boston: Shambhala, 1987.
Hanh, Thich Nhat. *Being Peace.* Berkeley, CA: Parallax Press. 1987.
——. *Old Path, White Clouds: Walking in the Footsteps of the Buddha.*
    Berkeley, CA: Parallax Press, 1998.
Kornfield, Jack. *A Path With Heart: A Guide Through the Perils and Promises of
    a Spiritual Life.* New York: Bantam, 1993.
Moody, Harry R. and David Carroll. *The Five Stages of the Soul: Charting the
    Spiritual Passages That Shape Our Lives.* New York: Anchor/Doubleday,
    1997.
Nisker, Wes. *Crazy Wisdom.* Berkeley, CA: Ten Speed Press, 1990.
Rahula, Walpole. *What the Buddha Taught.* New York: Grove, 1985.
Sahn, Seung. *Dropping Ashes on the Buddha: The Teachings of Zen Master Seung
    Sahn.* New York: Grove/Atlantic, 1987.
Salzberg, Sharon. *Faith.* New York: Riverhead Books, 2002.
——. *Lovingkindness: The Revolutionary Art of Happiness.* Boston: Shambhala,
    1995.
Suzuki, Shunryu et al. *Zen Mind, Beginner's Mind.* Trumbull, CT:
    Weatherhill, 1970.
Weisman, Arinna and Hean Smith. *The Beginner's Guide to Insight
    Meditation.* New York: Bell Tower, 2001.

Internet Resources

Buddhist information network. *www.buddhanet.net.*
Dharma Communications. *www.dharma.net.*
DharmaNet. *www.dharmanet.org.*
Insight Meditation Society. *www.dharma.org.*
Mountains and Rivers Order of Zen Buddhism. *www.mro.org.*
Quaker Church (Religious Society of Friends). *www.quakers.org.*
    Information about the central role of silence in Quakerism.
Sufi Dances of Universal Peace. *www.dancesofuniversalpeace.org.*
    A directory of times and places where Dances of Universal Peace are held.

The Kwan Um School of Zen. *www.kwanumzen.com.*
The Skillful Meditation Project. *www.meditationproject.com.*
Unified Buddhist Church and Parallax Press. *www.parallax.org.*
Vipassana Meditation. *www.dhamma.org.*Vipassana meditation as taught by
    S. N. Goenka is available on video via this Website.
World Wide Online Meditation Center. *www.meditationcenter.com.*

Mindfulness-Based Stress Reduction (MBSR)
The standardized eight-week course in Mindfulness-Based Stress
Reduction (MBSR) was developed through the Stress Reduction Clinic of
the University of Massachusetts Medical Center by Saki Santorelli and Jon
Kabat-Zinn. Facilitators taught by Santorelli and Kabat-Zinn offer
variations on the MBSR course in settings throughout the world. For
information, contact:
    Center for Mindfulness in Medicine, Health Care, and Society
    Univiversity of Massachusetts Medical School
    55 Lake Avenue No.
    Worcester, MA 01655
    (508) 856-5849
    www.umassmed.edu/cfm or *www.mbsr.com*

AUTHOR CONTACT INFORMATION

The author invites correspondence from readers on the subject
of this book. Contact him at *rmahler@newmexico.com* or in care of
Red Wheel/Weiser, 368 Congress Street, Boston, MA 02210-1864.